Is Small Business Ownership for You?

Is Small Business Ownership for You?

A Practical Guide for a Life-Changing Decision

By Laurie Johnson

BEP

BUSINESS EXPERT PRESS

Leader in applied, concise business books

Is Small Business Ownership for You?
A Practical Guide for a Life-Changing Decision

First published in 2025 by
Business Expert Press, LLC
222 East 46th Street, New York, NY 10017
www.businessexpertpress.com

ISBN-13: 978-1-63742-896-2 (paperback)
ISBN-13: 978-1-63742-897-9 (e-book)

Entrepreneurship and Small Business Management Collection

First edition: 2025

10 9 8 7 6 5 4 3 2 1

EU SAFETY REPRESENTATIVE
Mare Nostrum Group B.V.
Mauritskade 21D
1091 GC Amsterdam
The Netherlands
gpsr@mare-nostrum.co.uk

Description

Are you thinking about owning your own business, but wondering if this is the right path for you? Whether you are considering joining an existing firm as a principal owner, taking over a family business, starting up your own business, or buying an existing business, this book provides questions to contemplate as it walks you through *what it takes* from a personal aspect including:

- Traits
- Strategic Thinking
- Passion
- Relationships
- Commitments
- Cash Flow
- Risks and Rewards
- Timing and Exit Strategy

Readers will gain a real-life look into business ownership and learn *what owning a business is really like*. The author presents perspectives from other business owners gained through an interview process with 16 small business owners and shares some personal experiences. Many books have been written about how to start or run a business and others about specific topics such as leadership and management, but few address the personal aspects of small business ownership and the initial decision of, *Should I become a business owner?*

Acknowledgments

This book is a culmination of the efforts of many people. I would like to start by thanking all of those business owners who took the time to provide input through the interview process: Lisa Clark Balke, Sandra Belin, Chris Clifton, Ed Farr, Mike Hanson, Debby Hartman-Wrolson, John Hodgman, Larry Jacobs, Steve Johnson, Kristine Kubes, Cathy Mackenthun, Myron Moser, James Patrick, Bob Rehkamp, Charlene Roise, and Sue Stock. I would like to give acknowledgment and thanks to Charlene Roise and Steve Murray for content review and suggestions, David Gendreau for content suggestions, Kirsten Schwappach for proof reading, Sue Stock for final draft review, Perry Larson for review of the basics about commercial loans and lines of credit, Patti Bushnell for review of the basics about business insurance, Todd Strand for photography consultation, and Cherrie Bierley for the cover design. My husband Steve Johnson deserves special thanks for being a continuous sounding board and providing moral support, content review and photography for the book.

I would also like to thank Business Expert Press for working with me on this book, with special acknowledgment to Scott Isenberg, managing executive editor.

Testimonials

"It was very easy to go through the text, not something that I often find with books about business. I felt like the author was talking to me and had great insights to share …. This book should be very helpful for all of those crazy people out there wanting to own their own business—and I'm glad I was one of them."—**Charlene Roise, Historical Consultant and Former Owner of Hess, Roise and Company**

"If you are serious about owning your own business, you need to go in with your eyes open. Laurie provides key insights on what owning a business is like and how you prepare for the adventure. I would encourage all budding entrepreneurs to read this book to improve your chances for success."—**Steve Murray, President of Jet Edge (Retired), Small Business Investor and Turnaround Consultant**

"For anyone considering starting or owning a business, this book has a wealth of good information and questions to consider. The author addresses many of the 'You don't know what you don't know' kinds of things to be thinking about. I like the format, the Q&A section, and the personal stories."—**Sue Stock, Owner of COS and BEvera Executive Coaching**

Contents

Preface

What is it that makes someone want to own a business? And what is it really like? Business ownership is often portrayed as the American dream, but you can get in the weeds quickly without knowing what you are getting into. *Why did I do this and what did I get myself into?* often comes to mind.

My decision to become the majority owner of an existing business happened fairly quickly. I had come up through the ranks, starting at the company right out of college. One by one the founding partners were retiring or pursuing other interests, leaving an opportunity for those remaining. I knew that I either needed to take charge or leave the business. I talked over the decision with my spouse and several friends, receiving the encouragement to "Go for it." But honestly, I had no idea what I was getting into. That is the reason for this book. Based on my experience over the last 25 years, I can now share the knowledge I have developed and provide a guideline for making this life-changing decision of, *Should I become a business owner?* Take into consideration advice from others but understand that they don't have to do it, and you do. Do not expect others to be there for you when you need them. Do your due diligence and understand that this is about you.

The ideas for this book came about during the succession planning process for my business while holding training sessions for leadership groups. As I was fielding their questions and concerns, I realized that there are limited resources available to help potential owners wade through the decision of business ownership.

The need for this book was underscored during my interviews with other business owners. "I had no idea what I was getting into" is a common statement when talking with other owners. The personal aspects of business ownership are unknown for many, including what it takes to generate success and what owning a business is really like.

Introduction

Are you passionate about what you do, and do you think that you can do it better on your own terms? Have you identified a business opportunity that you would like to implement? Do you have an interest in acquiring and growing an existing business? Have you been asked to join an existing firm as a partner? Whether you are contemplating a start-up business, buying an existing business, joining an existing firm as a principal owner, or taking over the family business, the basic needs are the same. Successful business ownership requires long-term strategic thinking, the ability to make decisions, and resilience. An understanding of cash flow is crucial as well as having the financial capacity to weather the ups and downs.

This book walks you through important practicalities of business ownership that are seldom discussed, presents perspectives from other business owners gained through an interview process with 16 small business owners, and shares some personal experiences. Part 1 provides questions to ask yourself about key elements and considerations for owning and running a successful business. Consider the following questions:

- Am I determined and resilient?
- Can I make timely decisions?
- Can I provide the needed leadership?
- Am I good at solving problems?
- Do I have the confidence to initiate action?
- Can I apply strategic thinking to my business?
- Do I have a passion for the business?
- Can I develop and maintain the relationships needed to make my business successful?
- Am I willing to make the necessary time commitments to run a successful business?
- Am I willing to make the necessary financial commitments to run a successful business?
- Can I manage the business to provide a positive cash flow?

- Am I willing to take risks?
- Will business ownership provide the rewards that I need to make the venture worthwhile?
- Is this the right time for me to own a business?

Part 2 of this book shares a typical business management routine, shares some business ownership experiences, and provides responses to questions about business ownership to provide a real-life look into what it is like to own a business. This part is written in response to questions I have received over the years about what it is like to own a business, and the request for stories about my experiences. Consider these additional questions:

- Do the responsibilities and experiences of business ownership interest you?
- Do you believe that you are a good fit mentally and physically for the challenges that business ownership brings?

Part 3 guides you through your business ownership decision based on *what it takes* and *what it is really like*. Concluding remarks include reasons for business failures, the options for level of ownership, and the personal aspect of the opportunities and realities for starting a business, acquiring a business, joining an existing business, and taking over a family business.

Business owners were selected for interviews for this book to provide a broad-based perspective of small business ownership. The interviews include a mix of male and female owners, and start-up and existing business takeovers. The business sizes range from one employee or partner to 500 employees during some point of the business owners' tenure. Several of the businesses do not currently have employees, and several others have grown beyond the 500-employee threshold. Industries that are covered include manufacturing, distribution, professional services, construction, retail, agriculture, education, and hospitality. Qualifications for the interviews include successful business ownership for at least five years and a minimum of 20 percent ownership in the business. Owners who have significant business experience, the majority of whom have come full circle in either selling their business or are currently working on their exit, were selected. To simplify the narrative, those in this representative group will be referred to as the *owner(s)* hereafter.

Interviews were conducted to provide different perspectives and to identify commonalities and uniqueness among businesses. Advice from this representative ownership group includes the following:

- Dig deep to understand the real reason *why* you want your own business; do it for the passion and not for the money.
- Get industry related experience first; work and learn at another business.
- Do the research to understand the reality of what it will take; don't let anyone else talk you into it.
- Have a clear vision of what you want the business to be.
- Find a mentor and have a good support group.
- Make connections with other business professionals in your industry.
- Be willing to work hard and put in a lot of hours.
- Manage your money with care.

For the purposes of this book, use of the word *owner* assumes a minimum 20 percent ownership in the business with an active management role. This book does not address absentee ownership or passive investment as a limited partner. The words *partner* and *partnership* are used loosely throughout the book and do not imply a legal partnership. If you are contemplating being a principal owner in a business and taking a major role in running the business, then this book is for you.

This book does not tell you how to run or start a business. It provides thoughts and questions to contemplate, from a personal aspect, for those thinking about business ownership. Do you have what it takes, are you ready to make commitments, and do the rewards outweigh the risks?

PART 1

What Does It Take to Generate Success?

CHAPTER 1

Traits

Do you have what it takes to generate business success? Determination and a positive mindset, the confidence to make timely decisions, and the spirit to lead others are some key traits that are helpful in running a small business. The willingness to take the initiative and be proactive along with good problem-solving is also important. Some of these traits may come naturally to you and others may require substantial effort. Here is a starting point of questions that you can ask yourself.

Am I Determined and Resilient?

Running a business often feels like you are alone at the top, even when you have partners. Confidence, drive, and perseverance are needed to lead a business to success.

Do I Have Confidence in My Ability to Succeed and a Positive Mindset?

The number one mention for business success that surfaced during the interview process for this book involves mindset. All the owners that were interviewed agree that confidence or optimism is important in running a successful business. Statements such as, "You need to believe that the odds are in your favor," and "You need to believe that you can succeed," reiterate the importance of this. And then, "Know that what you are doing is right," and "Make sure your confidence is not misplaced."

Confidence in your abilities to run a successful business is of primary importance. If you don't believe you can do it, others won't either. Employees and customers will not want to work with you if they don't have belief in you and the business. Will employees want to work for you? Will customers want to engage with you? The importance of belief in yourself and belief in your mission and the future success of your company cannot be underestimated.

Are you an optimist or a pessimist? Overconfidence can get you into trouble. Too much focus on the negative will affect your attitude and reverberate throughout the organization and beyond. A realistic viewpoint with a focus on the positives will lead you down a path of success.

One owner talks about people finding excuses as to why not start their own business. "Most are not real," she says, "usually a sign they may not be a good fit to start their own business."[1] If you are looking for excuses, you do not have the mindset for business ownership.

Owner Feature

Cathy Mackenthun has been the owner of Mackenthun's Meats & Deli, Inc. since 1981. Her great grandfather started the business, and through her hard work, creativity, and leadership the business has thrived. She says that ideas come in the middle of the night and little by little she figured it out. After owning and operating the family business for over 40 years, she still enjoys going to work every day. There is "not a dull moment" she says. Cathy emphasizes the importance of patience, drive, and a positive attitude for business owners. She walks in every morning saying hello to her staff and calling them by name. She tries to compliment them and put a positive spin on things. "Don't walk in grumpy. Roll with it. Every day you have something new to try."

Am I Determined, and Willing to Put in the Effort Needed?

You are the one that must drive the business and make things happen. Excuses do not produce results. If you are not self-motivated or if you need reassurance and appreciation from others, then business ownership will not be easy for you. Friends and business associates may ask how the business is going and offer help, but your business will not be a priority for them and do not rely on them to be there. Employees

---

[1]Stock (2023).

expect you to care about them and guide them, but the reverse is not true. It is a rare employee who will ask the boss how they are or if they can help you.

Many of the owners point out the importance of personal drive and perseverance for business owners. You need the strength to stay on course. One owner cites the Calvin Coolidge quote, "Nothing in this world can take the place of persistence. Talent will not; nothing is more common than unsuccessful men with talent. Genius will not; unrewarded genius is almost a proverb. Education will not; the world is full of educated derelicts. Persistence and determination alone are omnipotent."

Seventy percent of the owners interviewed reference strong work ethic when asked about important traits for business owners. This includes comments such as, "Be willing to do whatever it takes," "You can't throw in the towel," and "Give it your all." One owner states, "First of all make sure it's something you love and second of all be prepared to not punch out for ten years," as he talks about working endlessly until you find success. "It took over ten years of taking the trash out,"[2] he says.

Am I Willing to Stand Up for What I Believe In?

Standing up for what you believe in is not the easy way out, but it will be impactful. You will earn respect, be proud of your business, and create a magnificent company culture for those whose beliefs align with yours. Doing what is right in everyday decisions, both internally and with customers, takes conviction. Compromises may be needed at times, but you need to be careful with this, choosing your fights wisely and keeping your focus on the big picture.

Multiple owners emphasize the need for trust, honesty, and good core values. "Without this, nobody will want to use you,"[3] one owner comments. You need to trust others and they need to trust you. Do you understand who you are and what you stand for? And can you keep your actions aligned with your values?

---

[2]Patrick (2025).
[3]Farr (2024).

Owner Feature

Mike Hanson was president and owner of Hunt Electric Corporation from 1996 to 2021, and he led the company through significant growth in his years at the helm. His business education includes a master of business administration (MBA) as well as having mentors in the former owner and other business professionals. Mike advises to build and diversify through integrity as he relays the negative effect of too much ego, no moral compass, and cutting corners. "I think it (integrity) makes it so much easier, and I think it makes your business more successful because people gravitate towards that ... We do what we say we are going to do. Everybody likes that. Now the tough thing about running a business is if that's the way you want to run a business and you're really committed to that, then you have to hold everybody else to that same standard too. Then you have to find customers that are willing to honor that, and you have to find people that are going to work for you to honor that, and the ones that don't you get rid of, whether it's a customer, an employee or a vendor."

"What you do makes a difference, and you have to decide what kind of difference you want to make."

—Jane Goodall

Can I Pick Myself Up When Things Go Wrong?

Are you resilient? Can you pick yourself up after rejection and when difficult issues arise? And can you lead and motivate others when you are down? You should not anticipate that everything will go smoothly, especially when you start out.

How do you manage stress? Will it keep you up at night when cash is tight and you have employees expecting a paycheck? How will you react to someone filing a lawsuit against your business? If you worry to the extent that you have trouble sleeping or tend to shut down and avoid issues you may not be well suited to business ownership.

A positive mindset and determination will go a long way in getting you through the difficulties, but you will also need to take care of your physical and mental health to have the capacity and energy to run the business. "In small business, you, as the owner and leader, are always needed. If you get sick, get hurt, etc., those relying on you may suffer as well. Consequently, you owe it to yourself to take care of yourself to ensure that you can be there, not only for yourself and your partner and family but for your clients and your team,"[4] one owner states. Another owner mentions the importance of mental health. "Don't do it (business ownership) if you are going through a big life change,"[5] she says.

Can I Make Timely Decisions?

Do I Have the Courage and Discipline to Make Timely Decisions That Are in the Best Interests of the Business?

If you have trouble making decisions or like to procrastinate, you will have difficulties in the business world. Putting off what needs to be done does not lead to success. Yet making rash decisions can also lead to difficulties. Take time to collect the necessary information, think through the impacts, and then make a decision and don't look back. Timely decisions keep the business moving forward and minimize financial, operational, and emotional stresses. If additional information becomes known later, you can make adjustments.

Collaboration with others can be extremely beneficial but it can lead you down a path that is not best suited for your business. Business owners need to be able to sort through input, weigh the pros and cons, and then make decisions themselves. Most decisions are not black and white or right and wrong. If the good outweighs the bad, move forward. One owner states, "Things need to move ahead in a timely manner, decisions made without fear of reprisal to instill ownership … but in the end the weight of the decision rests on your shoulders."[6]

Business owners are pulled in many different directions. Can you put aside the distractions and focus on the big picture decisions for the long-term good of the business? Several owners emphasize understanding

---

[4]Kubes (2025).
[5]Balke (2023).
[6]Belin (2024).

the big picture as an important trait for decision making. You need to be able to step back and look at the ramifications across all areas of the business. Some decisions will be difficult—think about firing employees, changing direction after you have invested time and money, and turning down work from customers that are not a good fit for the business. Pleasing everyone is usually not an option. You need courage and discipline to make decisions that are in the best interests of the business, setting aside the personal interests of yourself and others.

Owner Feature

Steve Johnson joined Code Welding and Manufacturing, Inc. as a partner when the original founders were looking toward retirement. He was president and owner of the business from 2005 to 2022 and continues as an owner today after retiring from the day-to-day management. He learned the business basics through his master's in international management (MIM), but he credits most of his knowledge to the way he was raised—the value of money and the way to treat people. Steve emphasizes the need for confidence and good core values for business owners, and when making decisions being realistic and focusing on the big picture. "You need to be able to understand the details but always apply them to the big picture because you can get lost in the trees pretty easily and waylaid," he says. Any time issues come up he thinks, "What are the unintended consequences and what's the big picture effect?"

"Don't let the noise of others' opinions drown out your own inner voice. And most important, have the courage to follow your heart and intuition."

—Steve Jobs

Do I Have Sound Judgment?

Good judgment comes from knowledge and experience, and the ability to balance risk with constraint. The importance of self-awareness and understanding what you do and don't know was voiced by many of the owners. Mentions include humility, honesty with yourself, and candor. You don't know everything, and you need to know when to reach out to others for help. You need to be "grounded in who you are," one owner states, and "understand your limitations."[7]

"You are a product of your work experience,"[8] another owner states as he relays the importance of your experience. If you do not have experience in business, management, and the industry, do you have the capital to get you past some mistakes due to bad judgment? Mistakes can be valuable learning tools, but they can also be costly.

Can I Provide the Needed Leadership?

Can I Inspire and Motivate Others and Myself?

Do you have a passion for the business, the desire to learn, and enjoy a challenge? If your answer is yes, you should not have difficulty inspiring and motivating yourself. But can you share this spirit with others? Can you get out in front of people and express your passion, desires, and challenges? Leadership is about people—communicating with them, caring about them, understanding them, respecting them, and having faith in them. This applies to everyone that will touch your business—customers, employees, vendors, and consultants.

Can I Convey My Big Picture Ideas and Solutions to Others?

Are you a clear communicator and consistent in your message to others? Do others trust that you will do what you say you will do? Can you admit when you don't know something, or do you let your ego get in the way? Good leaders develop trust and respect and are good communicators. To get others on board with your goals, you need to clearly convey your ideas and develop belief through consistency, honesty, knowledge, and

[7]Stock (2023).
[8]Rehkamp (2025).

experience, and then lead the way by setting an example through your own actions. You need to "live and breathe your business to realize your vision,"[9] one owner states.

Can I Develop a High-Performance Team and Keep Them Working Toward a Common Goal?

Can you develop a team of people that believes in you and your business goals? Leadership involves understanding others' strengths, needs, and vulnerabilities so that you can encourage, teach, support, and motivate them. Are you approachable, a good listener, and open to feedback so that others can vet out their questions and concerns? Are you flexible enough to allow outside input while not straying from the desired path? Can you provide guidance without stifling creativity?

One owner emphasizes the importance of teamwork with the following statement, "If you are going to do this, you need to form a team because no matter how good you are at one thing, to really make an efficient small business work requires more than even two or three really smart people that need to be very different and cover the vast array of skill sets that are required to be successful."[10]

Many of the owners interviewed stress the importance of leadership, communication, and team building for business owners. Leadership training, choosing good people, and developing a good team were all mentions that helped to lead these owners to success, especially among the larger businesses.

Leadership is about making an impact with others and leading change, when necessary, not just maintaining the status quo. Can you get others to change their course of action and then keep them on track and hold them accountable? It takes patience, courage, and tenacity to keep others on track with your goals.

"A leader is one who knows the way, goes the way, and shows the way."

—John C. Maxwell

---

[9]Belin (2024).
[10]Patrick (2025).

Am I Good at Solving Problems?

Do I Enjoy the Process of Resolving Problems and Taking Responsibility for the Solutions?

Business provides a continuous array of issues and, as an owner, you will need to identify problems and provide solutions. In his book *What It Takes*, Charles D. Ellis states "Great organizations spot troubles early and act against them decisively."[11]

Am I Good at Investigating, Figuring Out Options, and Then Extrapolating Out the Impacts?

Problems can surface both internally and externally involving human resources, marketing, operations, and finance. One of your employees may be affecting morale, you may have too much inventory, or your competitors may be taking some of your customers. Investigating takes basic knowledge in all areas of the business to know what questions to ask and the thoroughness to uncover the root of the problem.

Figuring out options takes creativity balanced with practicality. Can you innovate to come up with solutions that differentiate you from your competitors and turn the negative into a positive? Maybe you can start a training program, update your packaging, or change your price structure. Will you be able to view problems as opportunities for change and improvement? Innovation and creativity were brought up in the interviews as key components to solving problems. "It's important to continuously innovate to be competitive and ahead of your competition,"[12] one owner states.

Weighing the impacts of each option requires foresight. Can you extrapolate out the potential solutions to predict both short-term and long-term ramifications across all areas of the business? What may be a positive for your employees may have a negative effect on your customers or finances. The solutions may need to be a balancing act to avoid negative

---

[11]Ellis (2013), 181.
[12]Jacobs (2024).

impacts to one specific area of the business. You will need to look at the big picture to decide which solution is best for your business.

If you enjoy the problem-solving process and you can connect the dots to provide a glimpse into future consequences, then you will enjoy the challenges of problem-solving that business ownership brings.

Numerous owners refer to problem-solving as a valuable trait for running a successful business—the ability to overcome obstacles and learn from your mistakes, and being flexible yet still able to maintain your path. One owner verbalizes this well with her statement, "Embrace serendipity and use this as stepping-stones to learn and adapt."[13] Deal with issues head on. Learn from your mistakes but don't dwell on them. Forward thinking is critical for a successful business. "Take a problem, find a solution."[14]

Can I Negotiate to Provide the Best Solutions for the Business?

Negotiation is a powerful tool for business owners. Many problems can be resolved by negotiation. Think about negotiating with customers and vendors on contract terms, scope of work, schedules, and pricing; with

---

Owner Feature

John Hodgman founded his printing and direct mail business, Direct Connection, in 1990 and then purchased another company several years ago to double the size of his business. His business degree helped him with basic business knowledge, but he learned work ethic from his dad. John says that business is his passion, and he figured it out as he went along. Working in the industry for a friend sparked starting his own business with the "if he can do it, I can do it" mentality. John talks about the need to be driven and to be willing to work hard. "I think it's much more about your drive and attitude than your knowledge," he states as he relays some of the setbacks he has faced over his 35 years of business ownership and the need to keep trying and pushing forward. "Try not to be scared of what you don't know," he says.

---

[13]Roise (2023).
[14]Mackenthun (2024).

employees on salaries and training; or with banks on interest rates and terms for your loan. Most things are negotiable. Do you have the communication skills needed to be a good negotiator? Are you open-minded to consider other perspectives yet able to stay calm and focused on the needs of the business? Negotiation is a skill that can be learned, but having the right traits will go a long way in making you an effective negotiator.

Do I Have the Confidence to Initiate Action?

Can I Act Quickly to Take Advantage of Opportunities, Follow Through on Decisions, and Implement My Ideas?

Being proactive is a valuable trait to have in business. If business owners wait to react they will not be setting their own direction but letting others do it for them. An owner needs to be able to "manage their own narrative."[15]

Decide what you want and go after it. It is amazing what you can do when you set your mind to it. This includes everything from pursuing new customers and opportunities to making sure your invoices are paid in a timely manner. If you don't act quickly when an opportunity arises, your competitors will pounce and leave you wanting. If you don't make cuts in staffing or expenses as soon as downward trends are noted, your profits will disappear. Delays in contacting a customer to find out why they are not paying your invoice may result in others getting paid before you or not getting paid at all. You need to start the ball rolling to make things happen. Can you quickly initiate action after you make a decision, or do you hesitate, fearing the unknown or negative reactions?

Some people are good at coming up with ideas, others are good at making decisions, and others are good at taking action and implementing ideas and decisions. Few people are good at all three. Where do your strengths lie? One owner describes an adept business owner as "the type of person who is observant, takes initiative, has fire in the belly and an anxious edge, and inspires problem-solving."[16] She goes on to provide an

---

[15]Kubes (2025).
[16]Belin (2024).

example of a young intern that could walk into the room, see what was needed, and act on it versus a long-term employee that was more comfortable waiting to be told what to do.

Do I Have the Desire to Drive Performance, or Am I More Comfortable Maintaining the Current Situation and Not Ruffling Feathers?

Most people do not like change. Leading a company to success requires confidence, forward thinking, and the guts to act on it. It may feel like you are swimming against the current or climbing a wall at times, but the path of least resistance does not lead to business success. If you are not comfortable being proactive, you may be better suited as an employee working for someone else.

The importance of timeliness and taking action for business owners was brought up by many of the owners with mentions of not being complacent and not being a procrastinator. One owner discusses the sense of urgency that is needed, "Some things need to get dealt with right now, and some things are not fun. It's not all sunshine."[17]

"Drive thy Business, let not that drive thee."

—Benjamin Franklin

---

[17]Johnson (2023).

CHAPTER 2

Strategic Thinking

Strategic thinking is big picture thinking. It is about stepping back to consider the possibilities and figuring out a path forward for the long-term success of the business. Some people may consider strategic thinking a trait and others a skill, but however you categorize it, the importance of this *thinking* for business owners cannot be slighted, and requires emphasis. It is not a one-time event but an ongoing thought process to set, maintain, and adjust the direction for your business.

Can I Apply Strategic Thinking to My Business?

Can I Organize My Thoughts, Sorting Through the Potential Opportunities and Hurdles, to Develop a Plan for Implementation and Long-Term Growth?

Some people seem able to think through these strategic questions and others struggle to see the big picture. If you are not good at strategic thinking, consider hiring a consultant to walk you through an initial strategic planning process to develop a business plan. A business plan provides a guide for moving forward and efficiency of thought, defining what is important and where you should be spending your time to achieve the desired outcomes.

Start thinking through these questions:

- What is the market for my product or services and how will I deliver what the customers need or want?
- What is the competition, and why will customers choose my business over theirs?
- What is the required capital expenditure for start-up/acquisition as well as operations, and where will I get these monies?

- Will the business generate the profits that I need to make the venture worthwhile?
- What can I do internally and what will I need to outsource?
- What are the risks and how will I react and manage them?

These questions are a good first step in determining if you have a viable business.

Can you establish an ongoing strategic thinking pattern for yourself to plan, apply, and adjust your business strategies? Some people will need to schedule a weekly time for this deep thinking, others will be able to do it continuously or as events happen. If strategic thinking does not come naturally to you, you may want to develop a list of high-level questions to help you focus on big picture marketing, financial, and operational objectives.

According to the *Forbes Advisor* Small Business Statistics, "For a small business to be successful, it's imperative not only to have adequate capital to sustain operations in the early stages but also to ensure there is a consistent and growing demand for its product or services."[18]

Can I Align the Business Goals with My Personal Goals?

Outsiders often want to measure your success based on growth, number of employees, or revenue. This may not be in line with your vision. A common goal among the owners of the smaller businesses is simply to do what they love on their own terms. Taking the time to think through your personal values, why you want to own a business, and what you want to get out of the business is a key step to setting the pace and tone of the business.

- What are my goals for the long-term growth of the business, and do they match my bandwidth?
- How will my personal monetary needs and desires affect the fiscal management and growth of the business?
- How will the company culture reflect my values?

---

[18]Main (2024).

Can you apply these personal aspects to your business plan so that your goals are aligned?

Owner Feature

Sue Stock used her experience in architecture and construction to start COS, Inc. in 1997 providing owner representation for health care construction projects. This led to the founding of two additional businesses focusing on team building, leadership development, and coaching. Sue is a lifelong learner and attributes her business education to mentors, her can-do attitude and the school of hard knocks. She emphasizes the importance of strategic thinking, planning, and networking for business owners. She says, "Have a vision for the business. Be clear about the values and the environment you want. Plan out your business, have a strong vision, strong values, and create a culture that supports both, and then make sure you bring in clients that align with these; this will be an important piece of how successful you will be." She also advises, "Have a clear understanding, and be specific in defining what success means for you."

Can I Think Locally, Regionally, and Globally to Forecast Changes, Needs, and Impacts to the Business and Customers in the Next Year, in 5 Years, and in 10 Years?

Forecasting is an important part of strategic thinking. Can you anticipate, adjust, and innovate to keep the business on a successful path? You need to be able to see what's coming and what will be needed to move your business ahead.

Questions to contemplate include:

- What advances in technology are anticipated and how will they impact my business and customers?
- Could changes in legislation (taxes, tariffs, funding, codes, etc.) impact my business or customers?
- What will happen to the industry in an economic downturn?
- Are there social or cultural trends that will affect my employees or customers?

These questions can be part of your ongoing strategic thinking to make sure the business is on track and adapting to changes. Businesses and their environments are living things. They do not stand still. Constant learning, change, and adaptation are required to be successful.

Multiple owners pointed out the importance of forecasting and adaptability for business owners with comments such as the need to "keep up with the times," "anticipate what's needed," and "be flexible." One owner provides an example of a fourth-generation florist that didn't adjust his business strategies when the United States started importing flowers from South America. The business ultimately failed when it didn't adapt to the changes in the industry.

"We always overestimate the change that will occur in the next two years and underestimate the change that will occur in the next ten. Don't let yourself be lulled into inaction."

—Bill Gates

Basics to Know About Business Plans

A business plan is a document that outlines the company's vision, mission, and values. Key components to the plan may include a mission statement, goals, strategies for implementation, description of products and services, value proposition, competitive advantages, target markets and marketing strategy, financial projections, cash flow and required investments, information about the company organization and management, and company culture. There are many standard templates available for these plans.

A business plan is typically written with a three-to-five-year timeline and should be reviewed and updated on an annual basis. Plans should also be updated when major changes are occurring either internally or externally that will affect your business.

Banks and other investors often request business plans prior to providing funding. Business plans can also be a valuable tool for owners to define and track their business objectives and to share this information with their employees and other relevant parties.

CHAPTER 3

Passion

Passion is an interesting subject that came to the surface when 90 percent of the owners interviewed brought up the importance of passion for running a successful business. I had originally addressed passion in several of the other chapters of the book, as passion affects almost everything you do. But after hearing the importance that the owners placed on passion for business owners, it was added as a chapter to the book for emphasis. The owners call it "the fire inside." They talk about the need for business owners to go above and beyond; you need to do it for the love or desire of what you are doing and align the business with your passions. Passion provides the motivation to keep you going. "It gets you through the struggles,"[19] one owner says.

Do I Have a Passion for the Business?

Do you have a passion for your industry, a passion for your ideas or business goals, a passion for business itself, or a passion for a part of the business? Or maybe you are just a passionate person in general. Passion is the emotional part of running a business. Running a business without passion is like listening to a technical musician that does not have a feel for the music. It comes across as flat and uninteresting. Owning a small business requires constant effort and can be daunting and wearisome without passion. Passion keeps you hopeful with anticipation. Passion provides the energy and excitement that you need to run the business and it will attract others to your business. Employees, customers, and vendors will want to be a part of your team.

---

[19]Hartman-Wrolson (2023).

Do I Have a Passion for the Company Mission?

Some owners have a passion for the big picture mission of the business such as having a product or service that provides value to the community or improves the lives of the customers or employees. This passion tends to run deep, providing a purpose to their life and work. If you can align the company mission with your primary beliefs and values, this will provide the drive and enthusiasm that you will need to lead a business to success.

Owner Feature

Larry Jacobs and Sandra Belin cofounded Jacobs Farm, Inc. in 1980, one of the early certified organic farms in the country, and expanded to include the Del Cabo collective in 1985. Family support was instrumental in getting the business started. They had both worked on farms; Larry has an agricultural degree and took a few accounting courses, and they learned as they went along. They convey their passion for the business when they talk about helping people and loving what they are doing. *Healthy soils, healthy plants, and healthy people* is their mission. After 45 years, Larry can still say, "It doesn't feel like a job when you are doing something that gives you satisfaction." Larry and Sandra advise that being passionate and believing in your mission helps distinguish your product and motivate your team.

Do I Have a Passion for Business Management?

Some owners have a passion for the challenges of running and growing a successful business, including the business planning, finances, and management. Several of the owners have been passionate about business since they were kids, majoring in business in college, and then intentionally pursuing business ownership where they found opportunities.

Do I Have a Passion for the Industry?

Many of the owners have a passion that leans more toward a specific industry such as manufacturing or construction where their interests lie.

Some of these owners have come up through the ranks of the business, joining the company's ownership group and then working their way up to the top. Others have started their own business or acquired a business in their chosen industry. I can hear the passion in their voices as they share their enthusiasm for their company and the industry.

Do I Have a Passion for the Specifics of What I Will Be Doing?

Others yet have a passion for the specifics of what they do and what it brings to them personally. Several owners mention the need to be an expert at part of the business, whether it is sales, operations, technical, or another area of the business. Most accountants love their accounting, engineers and architects love their design, and attorneys love their lawyering. Other owners expressed their passion in working with their customers or working with their employees. What is your area of expertise, and is this a passion that you can bring to the business?

The application of passion to the business varies between the owners, but the importance of business owners having a passion for the business was highlighted in most of the interviews. You do not need to have a passion for all areas of the business, but the more aspects of the business that you can align with your passions the better off you will be. If you don't consider yourself a passionate person, you may want to think in terms of your interests, beliefs, and values.

If you don't enjoy the management part of business why would you want to own and manage a business? Many of the owners convey their enjoyment of business with statements like "Business is fun" or "Business is exciting," but business management is not necessarily their primary passion. Several admit their dislike of a particular part of the business such as accounting or managing people; however, they understand the importance of this function and have figured out how to address it.

Why would you want to own a business in an industry that doesn't interest you? Some of the owners are not necessarily passionate about their industry, as their experience and the opportunity led them to where they are, yet they are moderately interested in the industry. One owner states that he would not get into a business that didn't interest him.

The importance of belief in your mission cannot be understated, but a passion for business, the industry, and the specifics of what you will be doing are also important. All the owners have aligned the business with their passions in some way or another.

Where do your passions lie? And can you apply these passions to the business?

Owner Feature

Myron Moser, principal owner of Hartfiel Automation, Inc. from 2000 to 2021, led his distribution business through significant growth with his strong leadership. With a technical background in fluid power engineering, his business expertise is attributed to spending time with successful people and an executive leadership program. He associates his success with taking risks, finding the right people, and then putting them in the right positions. Myron emphasizes the importance of passion, perseverance, and trust-based relationships. He advises to understand your aptitudes, temperament, values, and interests, and choose your business based on these. "Someone that is not passionate about their profession—that would be drudgery, it would be fear, it would be stress." You need to "feed your geek" he says.

"Enthusiasm is the yeast that makes your hopes shine to the stars. Enthusiasm is the sparkle in your eyes, the swing in your gait. The grip of your hand, the irresistible surge of will and energy to execute your ideas."

—Henry Ford

CHAPTER 4

Relationships

Owning a business may seem like an independent venture but engaging with people and being able to develop solid relationships with partners, customers, consultants, vendors, and employees will be central to your business success.

Being a people person is considered important to some of the owners, while another owner mentions the number of introverts that are successful business owners. "There are a lot of entrepreneurs that are quiet and unassuming,"[20] he says. Several of the owners affirmed the importance for business owners to get in front of people and engage with them. For introverts, they need to "push beyond a natural instinct to hide in a closet,"[21] one owner states.

When business owners were asked what relationships have been the most important to them and their business, the responses varied from spouse and friends to partners, industry and business peers, employees, customers, vendors, and professional consultants and advisers.

> "If there is any one secret of success, it lies in the ability to get the other person's point of view and see things from that person's angle as well as from your own."
>
> —Henry Ford

Can I Develop and Maintain the Relationships Needed to Make My Business Successful?

Have I Considered Business Partners?

Think through the pros and cons of going into business with others. Partners can help to distribute responsibilities and commitments, provide valuable insight and support, and help to offset any weaknesses that you

---

[20]Clifton (2023).
[21]Roise (2024).

may have. They can also be a source of stress and misery. Before entering a partnership, ask the following questions:

- What is their financial history? Have they filed for bankruptcy or defaulted on a loan? Are they good at managing their personal finances?
- What strengths will they bring to the business? Do their traits, knowledge, and experiences complement yours?
- Do you trust this person and do your core values align? And do you have the same goals for the business?

Develop a written ownership agreement to document the key rights and responsibilities for each owner and establish terms for investment and sale of the business. Partnerships often end in quarrels if terms are not agreed to up front and documented in writing. What may be an amicable relationship at the start can change quickly with the realities and stresses of business ownership.

Partnerships and marriages have much in common. They are both relationships that take effort, and synergy is important. You need to support and motivate each other, hold each other accountable, and cover for each other when required due to workload, vacation, sickness, or other issues. I have found that you should not assume anything. It is best to establish weekly communications, ask questions, and follow up in writing to make sure you agree on critical issues and decisions. You will want to learn how to best work with them, what they can and cannot do well, and appreciate what they contribute.

Seventy percent of the owners interviewed started out with partners in their initial ownership venture. Forty-five percent of those that started out with partners transitioned to sole ownership.

Multiple owners have experienced difficult partnerships, some ending with resentment and conflicts that required attorney involvement. The owners advise to be brutally honest with yourself when evaluating a potential business partner and get a good attorney to draw up an ownership agreement. Move forward with caution and be prepared for the partnership to unravel. One owner relates selecting partners to his music industry with his quote, "If you are really good at playing piano, don't start a band with someone who's really good at playing piano."[22]

---

[22]Patrick (2025).

Owner Feature

Lisa Clark Balke has owned Victory Vintage LLC, a boutique home décor store, with a long-time friend since 2015. They learned the ropes of the industry at a previous employer, and they divide up management responsibilities based on each of their strengths. Lisa stresses the importance of partners. She states, "It is a big difference if you have a partner or not. You can play off each other—chemistry is key." She and her partner complement each other, provide "someone to bitch to and bounce ideas off," and are still going strong after 10 years in business together. Her advice to business owners includes having a unique sense of identity and knowing your target audience. "Know the lingo of what you are doing" and "educate your customers."

Basics to Know About Ownership Agreements

Ownership agreements, depending on the legal structure of the business, may include shareholder agreements; corporate bylaws; operating agreements; or partnership agreements detailing the roles, rights, and responsibilities for each owner, or board of directors and officers, as applicable. These plans can define items such as capital investments, decision making, signing authority, compensation, benefits, dividend policies, communications, buyout provisions, and the dispute resolution process when disagreements occur.

Buy–sell agreements or shareholders' agreements, common in corporations, define how stock shares will be purchased and redeemed including price, terms of payment, what happens when owners die or their employment is terminated, along with restrictive covenants such as confidentiality and noncompete.

Attorneys typically draw up ownership agreements specific to your needs and desires. Standard templates are available as a guideline but note that state statute requirements vary.

Ownership agreements can be supplemented with a more personal owners' plan (a counterpart to the business plan) to cover the owners' expectations and values including items like reinvesting profits in the business, owner distributions, tolerance for taking on debt, and exit strategies including ownership transfer to a next generation as applicable. Cary Tutelman and Larry Hause explain owners' plans in depth in *The Balance Point.*[23]

Do I Have Customer Relationships That I Can Tap Into?

If you currently do not have customer relationships, you will need to develop these quickly to get the business producing a revenue stream. As the owner, you will be the face of the company, and your actions and words will set the tone. Can you reach out to customers, listen to their needs, develop a level of trust, and determine if they are a good fit for your business? Knowledge and trust of your customers is invaluable, and their knowledge and trust of you is equally valuable. Think through the pros and cons of each potential customer. Get referrals and do research before entering into a contract. Questions that you can contemplate include:

- Is this customer trustworthy and do your core values align?
- What is their financial history? Do they have any judgments filed against them?
- Are their payment terms acceptable?
- What are their needs and expectations, and can you meet them?
- Can they provide referrals?
- Are there opportunities to develop a long-term relationship with this customer?

It is easy to say yes when work lands at your doorstep, but if the customer is not a good fit for your business or is not trustworthy, you will be better off not taking the work.

Customers are much like partners. You need to learn how to best work with them, develop an understanding of each other, and appreciate what they bring to your business. Synergy and support of each other is

---

[23]Tutelman and Hause (2008), 74–89.

important. Do not assume anything. Communicate, ask questions, and document everything in writing to make sure you agree.

Most of the owners cite the importance of customer relationships. One owner portrays the sentiment well with his statement, "Client relationships are everything. If you go in and buy a business at noon on Monday, by 12:30 that day you need to be in your biggest client's office making sure that relationship is solid."[24]

Another owner emphasizes the importance of customer relationships with his question, "Who do we know?" when they are pursuing new work. If they do not know the engineer, owner, developer or general contractor, they are not going to bid it. Taking care of existing customers takes priority. "Practice saying no," he says.[25]

This thought is furthered as one of the owners discusses choosing your customer base carefully. "Inform your gut and then listen to your gut … Sometimes your best business decision is no."[26]

Do I Have a Support Group?

Everyone needs support. Your support group should include friends and family who align with your business commitment and can provide encouragement and moral support. Several owners emphasize the importance of having the right significant other. "It helps if your life partner appreciates what you are doing … they understand what you are trying to accomplish, and support you rather than resent you,"[27] one owner states.

Other business owners or knowledgeable business people to talk with and provide insight are also critical components of your support group. Do you have at least one mentor or respected adviser? Finding a mentor or adviser that understands business, your industry, and that you respect, trust, and has the same values as you is ideal. It is possible that a partner could fill this role, but an outside perspective is always good. Ninety

---

[24]Clifton (2023).
[25]Hanson (2025).
[26]Kubes (2025).
[27]Ibid.

percent of the owners talk about the importance of support and someone to discuss business matters with. One owner says, "You need people that will tell you the truth."[28] Another states, "You are somewhat isolated. You need to talk with others you respect. You need someone that you can ask if you are in left field."[29]

Support groups were brought up by many of the owners. They emphasize the benefits of involvement in chief executive officer (CEO) programs and industry-based peer groups to provide a network of people with business experience for an outside viewpoint. One owner talks about joining groups, throwing yourself on the mercy of others when you need help, and then giving back. "Get out there,"[30] she says.

There are many business networking groups that can be the starting point of establishing some great relationships. These include The Alternative Board (TAB); Vistage; Business Networking International; CEO roundtables; your local chamber of commerce; professional or trade associations; and online LinkedIn, Facebook, and Meetup groups. Another option is to find a business mentor through the Service Corps of Retired Executives (SCORE), a resource partner of the SBA (U.S. Small Business Administration).

Using a board of directors or board of advisers to provide expertise and to be a sounding board is another means of support. A board of directors, typical for corporations, can be set up unique to the needs of the business and include any combination of owners, family members, managers, and outsiders. Cary Tutelman and Larry Hause in their book *The Balance Point* detail out the possibilities for using boards. "The owners determine whether a board is needed, what it does, and who should be on it,"[31] they state. Including outsiders on the board can provide expertise, wisdom, and experience to help guide your business. A board of advisers is a more informal approach to get input and advice from outsiders.

---

[28]Stock (2023).
[29]Johnson (2023).
[30]Roise (2023).
[31]Tutelman and Hause (2008), 176–196.

Owner Feature

James Patrick, who is on his third business venture as cofounder of Slam Academy LLC in 2012, attributes his business education to learning by doing it the wrong way. He highlights the importance of relationships with other people who are better at things than he is, crediting his success to forming a good team and developing mutually beneficial industry connections. "Community and networking with like-minded industry professionals is huge," he states and goes on to provide examples. "The music school became great when it connected with the right software companies and the right musical instrument companies who believed in our business and wanted to support us … The musical instrument companies want our student's business and I want the credibility of having their logo on our website and being endorsed as an official place to teach their technologies."

Do I Have Connections to Help Me Develop a Trusted Professional Network?

Independence is a necessity, but it is important to develop a network of professionals to provide the resources and expertise that you will need. Your network of key people may include outside expertise in legal, accounting, marketing, banking, insurance, technology, and human resources. If you currently don't have a network of key people, you will need to make these connections. Referrals from family, friends, and industry associates are a good first step. You will need to develop a level of trust with some key people and then know when and how to use their expertise. Remember that you do not know everything. A good balance between doing your own research and reaching out to others has worked well for me.

Don Thompson, a management consultant, highlights the lack of business expertise in business owners in his article about avoiding the entrepreneurial syndrome. He states, "Very few entrepreneurs are people- or business-oriented. They have little or no training in these fields and consequently these areas do not get the time and attention required of a successful enterprise."[32]

---

[32] Thompson (n.d.)

A successful working relationship with consultants requires you to have some basic knowledge in the subject to provide direction and oversight. One owner stresses the importance of knowing *why* it is the right thing to do, and not just taking a consultant's word for it.[33] You need to be able to reflect back and ask yourself if it makes sense for you and your business. There should be mutual respect so that you can learn from each other and understand how to best apply their expertise to your business.

The majority of the owners emphasize the importance of a trusted relationship with a good accountant, and many of these owners name their accountant as an important mentor and adviser. Lawyers, landlords, insurance agents, bankers, and bonding companies were also named as essential relationships that can help contribute to success. Statements such as, "Don't skimp on professional advisors," and "Have people around you that know more than you do—to keep you out of trouble," were voiced by many of the owners.

The importance of banking relationships was highly variable among the owners, depending on the size and financial position of the business. Some just use basic banking services, but many highlight a banking relationship as one of the most important relationships for their business. These owners advise finding a bank that is a good fit for you. One owner states, "Deal with people that you trust—cultivate the relationship," as he reiterates a story about a larger bank calling in a loan on them. "They didn't want our business. You are more important to smaller banks. The larger banks are less willing to work with you."[34] Several owners recommend using a local credit union, especially in the first few years of a start-up business. As you establish your business and develop a good track record you position yourself to be able to move to a better banking scenario. Other owners found a good fit with a larger bank as their company grew but stress the importance of working with a decision maker at the bank.

Several owners mention using local and government resources to take advantage of free advertising and services. One owner took advantage of the SBA legal help, avoiding paying for her own attorney. The SBA offers

---

[33]Hanson (2025).
[34]Johnson (2023).

free or low-cost counseling as well as an online business guide (www.sba. gov/business-guide) with basic information on planning, launching, and managing a business that can be especially valuable for start-up businesses.

Owner Feature

Kristine A. Kubes, Esq. started her own firm, Kubes Law Office, PLLC, serving design and construction professionals, in 2009. She credits her business education to surrounding herself with good advisers and observing her parents in their construction business. She emphasizes the importance of good preparation and being courageous as well as having a good lawyer who is familiar with your particular area of business, a good accountant to set up your books from the beginning and whom you can call on with questions, an insurance adviser to get your insurance profile put together and whom you can bounce ideas off of as things arise, and for lawyers, an ethics adviser. Kristine conveys a principle that can be applied to many areas of life: "If you're in a crisis, that's not the time to begin creating your team. You need to build good relationships and have the team in place, so that when you need them, they are there."

Do I Understand My Competitors?

Developing relationships with your competitors is not the first thing that comes to mind for business owners, but some effort should be given here. Respectful relationships are the goal here. You need to understand as much as you can about what your competitors do and how they do it so that you can gain insight and remain competitive. In turn, you will need to reciprocate with information of your own. Guarded restraint is required with this, as you do not want to let them have the inside track on your business.

Competitor relationships can bring opportunities for collaboration and partnerships that you could not have on your own. You can pursue larger projects, develop new customer relationships, and learn from each other, but there can be unintended consequences and ulterior motives. Carefully weigh the pros and cons for your business prior to agreeing to a collaborative project. Teaming efforts can lead to being shut out of customer contact—losing the opportunity to develop a relationship and get the next project—and can take capacity away from other pursuits. And when times get tough or the budget runs out, the collaborative spirit can disappear leading to a situation where each business is left fending for themselves. You are the one that will need to make sure teaming commitments are in your best interest and align with your business strategy.

Do I Have Vendor Relationships That I Can Tap Into?

Knowledge and trust of vendors is just as important as knowledge and trust of customers. If you don't have these relationships, you will need to develop them. Depending on your business, vendors may be needed for materials, equipment, and/or labor. Vendors can tie up significant financial resources, and you will depend on them for quality work and timely delivery. They become part of your team. Fair pricing and payment terms will need to be negotiated. And as with customers, get referrals and do research before entering into a contract.

Multiple owners discussed the importance of good vendors and suppliers and building a level of trust with them. "They watch your back and look out for you,"[35] one owner states. Another owner says, "You can't force relationships that don't work," as he talks about the need to terminate relationships with customers and vendors that have unacceptable payment terms.[36]

Can I Keep My Employees Happy and Engaged?

Will you have employees in your business? If so, finding and developing the right team of people and then keeping them happy and engaged will be important.

Surround yourself with the best people that you can find with the same core values. Good ones are worth their weight in gold. Some people are great at following directions and completing tasks, while others are

---

[35]Hartman-Wrolson (2023).
[36]Johnson (2023).

thinkers and problem solvers. Both types of employees are important for a successful business. Hire to cover your weaknesses. Diverse knowledge and opinions is a good thing.

Happy and engaged employees means keeping everyone on a professional level with respect for all, providing opportunities and training to keep them challenged, and keeping them informed about the business. Can you listen, guide, and encourage them; give them credit for their contributions; and earn their trust?

When issues do arise, they should be addressed immediately. Will you be able to set parameters for acceptable conduct and skills? Can you be firm and fair? You will need to balance the needs of the employees with what is best for the business. Think about an analogy to football. If you want to win you will need teamwork, and you will need to get rid of those that do not perform or play by the rules.

Multiple owners attribute their business growth and success to finding the right people and putting them in the right positions. You need to "fill in what you're not an expert in," one owner says. "It's business killing if you don't have the right people."[37] Evaluation tools as well as gut instinct were cited as important for hiring and promoting the right people.

"Great things in business are never done by one person. They're done by a team of people."

—Steve Jobs

---

[37]Moser (2024).

CHAPTER 5

Commitments

How dedicated are you to making this a successful business? Both time and financial commitments should be considered.

Am I Willing to Make the Necessary Time Commitments to Run a Successful Business?

How Much Time Do I Have to Dedicate to the Business, and Will That Amount of Time Achieve the Results That I Am After?

Depending on the business and your expectations, the amount of time required for the business can vary significantly. But in general, business ownership is not an 8:00 a.m. to 5:00 p.m. weekdays only commitment. Be prepared to think about the business all hours of the day. Small businesses typically do not have the support staff to cover all the bases, so many times the choice is either you do it or it doesn't get done.

The time commitment of business ownership was highlighted many times in the interviews with statements such as, "Don't do it if you want a 9-to-5 job," "Be willing to wear many hats and work a lot of hours," and "It's like having a kid; it's 24/7." For several owners, the business is both their job and their hobby. They work on it every spare minute. One owner talks about being an architect by day and business manager by night. He says, "The time commitment is huge; always takes more time than you think."[38]

For many of us, business ownership is not just about work; it is a way of life. Business relationships and networking get intertwined with your personal life, and your best business advisers often end up being spouses or close friends. If you have high expectations, it can become all-encompassing figuring out opportunities and ways to improve. If you

---

[38]Farr (2024).

just want a job, and you are not dedicated to making your business and career a top priority, then business ownership is not a good fit for you.

Besides the day-to-day business operations, here are some time allocation needs for your consideration:

- Research and reading to obtain information, keep up on your industry, understand the external environment, and stimulate ideas.
- Consulting and networking with others to process ideas; come up with solutions; track your image and reputation; and develop connections, references, and referrals.
- Planning and strategic thinking to provide direction and focus. One's mind can run in endless circles, wasting huge amounts of time without direction and focus. Having blocks of uninterrupted time on a regular basis is helpful so that you can step back and think about the big picture. This can mean shutting the door of your office, going to the library or a coffee shop, or finding a quiet place at home or a cabin—wherever your thoughts and creativity are sparked.
- Dedicating time for employees. Employees are the lifeblood of the company, and it is important to spend time with them to keep them happy and all moving in the same direction. Employees can be the most challenging part of the business as well as the most rewarding part. Everyone is different, and it takes time to understand each one and keep him or her on track.
- Jumping when opportunities arise. Quick response is often the difference between a successful pursuit or not and typically means working extra hours at short notice.
- Handling emergency situations. Just when you think things are getting back to normal, something seems to happen. There is no normal in business. Both good and bad things happen that cannot wait. Your building may be vandalized, you have a good customer that needs help immediately, or maybe one of your employees is injured. It is true that some of these demands happen when you are an employee also, but ownership can put added weight to these demands. It is difficult to say no when you understand and feel the impact personally.

Business ownership requires a substantial time commitment. The time commitment can change as the needs of your business and life changes, but you will need to step up with additional effort when business issues and challenges arise.

Do you need a partner to share in the workload? Will you have a dependable person for backup, to cover vacations and other potential absences? Hiring the right staff, training, setting standards, and documenting processes and procedures can all assist in freeing up your schedule, but these take time to develop.

What Other Areas of My Life Require Time Commitments, and Can I Create a Workable Balance?

Each individual needs to decide the level of commitment they are willing to give to the business. Think through how your business commitments will affect your personal relationships and other important aspects of your life. The limited amount of time and energy and the need to make sacrifices, especially in the first few years, were mentioned by several of the owners.

Talk with your family. How will they feel about the additional time commitment required? Support and understanding from your family is invaluable. "Get 100% buy-in from your spouse and family,"[39] one owner advises. Another owner mentions the strain that business ownership can have on your relationship with a significant other. A third owner credits his spouse with taking on additional responsibilities at home to allow him to focus on his business.

Business ownership does allow you to work differently, but this does not mean you can work less. Your schedule can have flexibility, but it will be out of your control to a certain extent dictated by the needs of the business. If you are the type of person that is *all in*, friendships will transition to those that understand and support your business pursuits, and you may have less time for dating and significant others.

---

[39]Farr (2024).

Set limitations and expectations for yourself. Your physical and mental well-being is critical to maintain optimum performance in running your business.

> "I do not believe a man can ever leave his business. He ought to think of it by day and dream of it by night."
>
> —Henry Ford

Owner Feature

Debby Hartman-Wrolson acquired the St. Boni Bistro in 2017 and continued to own and operate it for seven years until the recent sale. Her dedication, creativity, and hard work enabled her to grow the restaurant during the challenging years of the COVID-19 (coronavirus disease 2019) pandemic and make it into a community destination. Debby came from an entrepreneurial family and worked in the family business but ventured out on her own for an opportunity that followed her passion to provide healthy organic food. She talks about the 110 percent commitment required and needing someone you can trust while you take a vacation. She advises keeping an open mind and taking baby steps; it takes time. "It looks easy from the outside," she says. "Leave the business at the end of the day—don't give up your life."

Am I Willing to Make the Necessary Financial Commitments to Run a Successful Business?

Do I Have the Money Needed for the Initial Investment in the Business?

How much cash will you need for your initial investment in the business, and where will you get this cash? If you are buying into an existing business as a partner, this may be a personal equity investment that you may not see return on until you sell the business. If you plan to borrow money from a bank or other third party, do you have the cash needed to make the required down payment? And are you comfortable with the terms and payback schedule for the loan?

The initial financial commitments required from the owners ranged greatly. For some it was *all in*, meaning selling their house and using their retirement and college funds for kids to put together an initial down payment on a business and then running a highly leveraged business. Others had family financial support or were small start-ups that required little financial investment. One owner financed the purchase of two different businesses through the Small Business Administration (SBA) 7(a) loan program. This program allows for a low down payment and provides the opportunity for financing beyond the hard asset value of the business. Another owner used seller financing for both his initial business purchase and for acquisitions to expand his business.

Many of the business owners relayed the financial struggles of the initial years. "You are in a survival mode," they said. For some the money was better after the first few years, for others it took 10 years, and another 25 years, to get to that position.

Do I Have the Financial Resources to Back a Line of Credit or Loan? And Am I Comfortable Pledging My Personal Assets for the Business?

In addition to your initial investment, how will you fund your ongoing business operations? Getting a loan or a line of credit from a bank typically requires anyone with 20 percent or more ownership in the business to personally guarantee the amount of the loan. This involves filling out a personal financial statement listing the assets that you own to back the loan or line of credit. If you have joint assets with a spouse or significant other, this should be discussed with them. Personal guarantees are also common for business accounts on many credit cards.

Do I Have Cash Reserves for Emergency Situations?

It is important to have some cash set aside for the business. It is great if you can cash flow your business without going to a bank, but this is rare. According to the *Forbes Advisor* Small Business Statistics, "Data shows that 38% of businesses fail due to exhausting their cash reserves or the inability to secure additional capital."[40]

Having cash reserves in your personal finances will allow you to keep the business moving along in difficult economic times without relying on credit cards or other high-cost credit that can quickly escalate out of control. A rule of thumb that I support is to pay yourself last. This keeps you out of trouble with vendors and the bank, and allows you to maintain your staffing during cash crunches. Can your personal finances support this, at least for a few months?

Several owners relayed the financial struggles during a recession and the need to take salary cuts, withhold pay, and loan the business money to cover payroll by writing a personal check. The advice varied but with a consensus that when times get tight you need to cut your pay. You can only afford to pay yourself what is left after the bills have been paid. "You need to keep the lights on."[41]

Multiple owners mention the importance of keeping your personal finances separate from the business finances. Keep accounts separate, track expenses, and set up your personal loans to the business with interest payments, is advice from the owners.

What will happen if the business is not successful? Will you heed to the warning signs and not throw good money after bad? Understand your personal tolerance for financial risk and set limits on your financial commitments. Do you know how to move on? Twenty-five percent of the owners interviewed have experience with previous business ventures, some of which have not been overwhelmingly successful. You learn from your mistakes and with each venture you improve.

When working with a bank, make sure to read the loan and line of credit terms carefully and develop a relationship with your banker so that they understand the ebbs and flows of your business. In difficult times, they can call in the loan if the business is not meeting their financial requirements and seize personal assets if you default.

---

[40]Main (2024).
[41]Farr (2024).

Basics to Know About Commercial Loans and Lines of Credit

Banks set interest rates for commercial loans and lines of credit depending on the perceived risk of the loan and the strength of your financial situation. Interest rates can vary from 0.5 percent above the prime rate upward to 20 percent. Financial requirements in loan terms can include maintaining a specific debt service coverage ratio (ratio of available income to debt payments, including principal and interest). A minimum ratio requirement will typically range from 1.1 to 1.3. Other terms can include limitations on salary and/or distributions to owners as well as being first in line for seizing assets in case of a default. Both personal and business financial information will need to be submitted to the bank when applying for the loan and then at least annually thereafter. Qualifying for a commercial loan or line of credit with a bank as a start-up business may be difficult without several years of financial history. The Small Business Association (SBA) loan program may be a good option if you do not have the required financial history or do not meet other standard loan requirements of the bank. The SBA provides federal government backing for the loan, but it involves additional paperwork and fees.

A line of credit is typically established to cover fluctuations in cash flow (referred to as working capital) and is backed by your outstanding invoices (accounts receivable) or inventory. The amount of your credit line will typically be limited to 75 percent of your account receivables that are under 90 days. The amount of an inventory-backed credit line will be limited to a percentage of the inventory value, depending on the type of inventory and sales history. Credit lines typically have annual renewals and are required to be paid down in full (rested) for 30 days each year. Interest rates for credit lines float with the prime rate.

Commercial loans are typically established for specific needs such as purchase of equipment or vehicles and are backed by those assets. The amount of the loan may be limited to 80 percent of the asset(s) value unless the SBA backs the loan. Commercial loans typically have a set term and either a fixed or variable interest rate. The bank may request a copy of your business plan, or other justification for the purchase(s). Commercial real estate loans for the purchase of a building typically run at higher interest rates than a residential loan for the purchase of a house and are shorter term. The term is often shorter than the amortization schedule requiring a balloon payment at the end, which often means refinancing after the set term.

CHAPTER 6

Understanding Cash Flow

One owner states, "Finance and accounting is the skeleton of business that supports everything. If you have an understanding of finance and accounting it's a big advantage."[42] This thought is furthered with many of the owners bringing up the importance of having a good accountant and "running tight books," as well as understanding taxes and how they will affect your business.

Several of the owners pointed out that money does not have to be the most important reason for owning a business, but it needs to be a primary focus. You need to be profit oriented. If you don't make money the business will fail.

Can I Manage the Business to Provide a Positive Cash Flow?

Business success and profitability are directly tied to cash flow. The basic premise is straightforward: The cash that comes in needs to be greater than the cash going out. This can be accomplished through both process control and budgeting, including everything from managing your staffing hours to saying no to expenditures that are not in the budget.

Do I Understand What It Will Take to Keep the Business in Motion?

The first component to cash flow is to understand the required processes and make sure they are timely and efficient. This includes getting customers in the door, getting the work done, and then making sure you get paid. Each step is important to maintain your cash flow.

---

[42]Clifton (2023).

1. Getting customers. This means jumping on opportunities, pushing relationship development and project pursuits to provide a workload that is balanced with your capacities. This also means making sure you are pursuing the right projects and trustworthy customers, accurately estimating your pricing, defining your deliverables, and negotiating favorable contract terms.
2. Getting the work done. This means monitoring progress, schedules, staffing, goods and materials, quality, and contract requirements; following procedures and standards; communicating issues and documenting changes; and getting the product delivered.
3. Getting paid for what you do. This includes timely invoices, monitoring payment status, and maintaining a collection process for past due invoices.

The understanding of operations and the effect it has on cash flow was reiterated in the interviews with statements such as, "You need to know what needs to be done to make it go," "You need to know how you make money," and "You need to know how cash flows through your business." Bottlenecks or inefficiencies in your process will slow down the flow of cash. Several owners brought up the importance of knowing every aspect of the business. An in-depth understanding of the processes and operations will allow you to identify bottlenecks and adjust priorities to keep the cash flowing. Mentions from the owners include figuring out the critical benchmarks for your company and monitoring your backlog to help predict the cash flow.

Do I Have the Discipline to Manage the Business Within a Budget?

A second component to cash flow is to manage within a budget. Forecasting a realistic annual revenue and then subtracting the desired profit is a fruitful exercise to provide you with a proposed annual spending budget.

The amount of detail in your budget is up to you, but make sure you have all the categories covered with an allowance for contingencies and bad debt. Budget categories include wages and benefits, rent and utilities, proposed purchases and supplies, training, licenses, loan and lease payments, interest payments, consultant fees, travel expenses, advertising, insurance, and taxes. If you can't balance the budget with your revenue forecast and profit goal, then you will need to dig deep and make adjustments. Will you need to reduce your salary or cut staff? Will you need to find a different building to save money on rent? Maybe you will need to delay a purchase or lease instead of buying. Developing a budget and then sticking to it is essential for good cash flow management.

"A budget is telling your money where to go instead of wondering where it went."

—John C. Maxwell

Owner Feature

Robert R. Rehkamp, CPA, took over an existing accounting firm in 1994, and he has had the opportunity to consult with many businesses over the last 30 years as he developed and grew his tax accounting business. Bob advises to follow your heart but take stock of your strengths and weaknesses. "Do you really have the desire to own a business ... or is it just a pipe dream?" he asks as he explains that it takes a lot more than a good idea—develop a financial plan and be prepared for the worst as revenue may not meet your goals. He talks through developing high/low forecasts and doing break-even analyses to answer the question, What do you need to get through? "Money is stressful; you live and die with your mistakes."

Can I Cash-Flow the Initial Business Investment?

If you plan to borrow money from a bank or other third party, how much cash will you need and how quickly will you be able to pay back the loan? It is important to understand the flow of cash through the business to answer these questions.

A monthly projection of cash in versus cash out is helpful to understand your cash flow and predict the cash that will be needed or available month by month. In addition to your initial investment, you will need cash (working capital) to cover the lag time from initial investment in inventory and labor to receiving payment from the customers. How much additional cash will you need to cover this lag? If you anticipate seasonal fluctuations, how much cash reserve will you need to cover those months with negative cash flow? And will you have money available if equipment breaks down or you want to make additional investments for a good opportunity? For a start-up business, cash flow projections will help to predict how long it will take until the business has a positive cash flow and when you can expect to generate profits. For an existing business, cash flow projections will help to predict how much profit you will generate and how long it will take to recuperate your initial investment.

Owner Feature

Edward Farr started his own architectural firm, Edward Farr Architects, Inc., in 1991. His enthusiasm, solid reputation, and organized approach have kept the business going for 34 years. He attributes his business ownership opportunity to being in the right place at the right time. He learned the ropes of business management while running a branch office for another company. When this branch office closed, he transitioned into his own business. Ed advises having family buy-in and ensuring that you can cash flow the business and repay a start-up loan. He states, "Know all of your initial investment costs and on-going operational costs to dial in your business plan financials. Interview owners of similar businesses to make sure you don't miss anything. Plan for success; but prepare for setbacks along the way. Always have a Plan B."

Financial management in small businesses is extremely important and usually done by the owner(s). Depending on the size of your business, you may have employees or consultants to provide some of the financial tasks and reporting, but owner oversight and decision making are critical for profitability and risk management.

Multiple owners relay the importance for business owners to understand financial statements. Financial statements not only indicate how the company is doing from a profit and loss standpoint but also provide a record of the past and a basis for budgeting and pricing your goods and services. Cash flow analyses are critical to predict the future and provide information that you need to set the priorities for the next few months. One owner talks about forecasting out the cash flow to understand future cash needs and to determine when the business is able to invest in future growth or automation.[43]

The probability of running a profitable business is low without a solid understanding of your cash flow.

---

[43]Jacobs (2024).

CHAPTER 7

Risks

"To win without risk is to triumph without glory."

—Pierre Corneille

Risks are an inherent part of business, and recognizing and managing the risks is an important part of running a business and keeping it financially viable. The definition of an *entrepreneur*, according to Webster's New Collegiate Dictionary and Oxford English Dictionary respectively, is "one who organizes, manages, and assumes the risks of a business or enterprise" and "a person who organizes and operates a business or businesses, taking on greater than normal financial risks in order to do so." You may not consider yourself an entrepreneur, but all small business owners need to take risks.

Am I Willing to Take Risks?

Can I Adapt and Change to the Outside Environment?

There are business risks that come from the outside world that are out of your control. There is little you can do about these risks except understand them, accept them as the risks in doing business, and adapt. Think about the impact of recessions, pandemics, riots, protests, strikes, government shutdowns, changes in programs and funding, tariffs, and changes in codes and regulations. Are you willing to take these risks?

Navigating changes in the economy and the ups and downs of your specific market is a difficulty that many of the owners have experienced. Discussions include knowing when to hire, fire, and work overtime hours; timing for expanding your building space; and dealing with sourcing and supply chain issues. Several of the owners point out the need for a stable market for your product to minimize risk. "Know that you have a dependable market, don't just hope,"[44] one owner states.

---

[44]Farr (2024).

Other owners mention the risks involved in dealing with changes in government regulations. One owner relays the challenges that increasing minimum wages brings for her labor-intensive business. Another owner talks about the risk his company faces when the government raises postage rates higher than inflation, driving demand down for his direct mail business. "As prices go up, you generally drive demand down,"[45] he says.

The amount of luck involved in business success was a topic that was brought up by several business owners. These owners agree that they have been lucky in that no catastrophic events happened to affect their success; but competency in management of the business puts the odds in their favor. "You can call it luck, you can call it good fortune, you can call it whatever, but generally it doesn't just happen,"[46] one owner states as he discusses reacting to major obstacles.

A second owner relates risk to betting on yourself. "Everyone can steer the ship when the weather is calm, but when things get rough, that's when you figure out who the real captain is in a company … that's where the real captain shows up and if they don't the ship goes down," he states.[47]

What is your risk tolerance? Do you get stressed when things don't go as planned or do you thrive on the challenge of the situation? One owner talks about the importance of understanding the level of risk you are willing to take and to pull back when you need to. "Give yourself bookends,"[48] he says.

Can I Manage Risks to an Acceptable Level Within My Inner Circle?

There are also business risks that happen within your inner circle. These are somewhat in your control and can be minimized through due diligence and good management as well as awareness, adaptation, education, and ingenuity. These risks can include changes in people, industries, financing, and technology; theft and cybercrime; errors, claims, and lawsuits; and issues with customers and employees. The person that you built a relationship with at your largest customer may leave his job, resulting in

---

[45]Hodgman (2024).
[46]Ibid.
[47]Moser (2024).
[48]Farr (2024).

you losing their business. A key employee may quit. You might purchase inventory for a product that doesn't sell. Your computer system may go down or you could have a security breach. You may be sued for poor performance, or your customer may go bankrupt.

Insurance can be purchased to cover some business risks. General liability, product liability, and professional liability along with coverage for property loss and cybercrimes are examples of insurance available to businesses. Depending on your industry, customers may have contractual requirements for specific insurance coverage. You will need to weigh the insurance costs with the value and risks for your business.

Security issues, computer issues, theft, and accidents are all something that most businesses will face. After experiencing physical break-ins, cybercrimes, computer server crashes, and vehicle accidents, I have found that the cost of insurance as well as enhanced security and training have been well worth the risks posed.

The risk of lawsuits is highly variable depending on the industry. Training, quality control processes, good documentation, and oversight can go a long way in minimizing your exposure to lawsuits, but some scenarios may be out of your control. Talk with your insurance agent about the specific risks for your business.

What about the risks that are not insurable? Virtually every decision you make as a business owner involves risk.

Financial decisions are of primary importance to managing risk. More debt can provide the dollars needed to invest in your business but relates to more financial risk. Another risk that many business owners will face is a customer who is not paying their invoices. Can you manage your finances to an acceptable level of risk?

For one owner, low overhead and product diversity have been the keys to managing risk. For others, customer selection, focusing on repeat business, and walking away from unfavorable contracts lowers their risk.

Lack of knowledge is another risk that looms for business owners. Staying up-to-date in your industry and the business world through networking, reading, seminars, and so on is relevant in minimizing risks. Up-to-date knowledge allows you to make more informed decisions and to be proactive in adapting to changes. Continual learning and adaptability are necessary.

An advisory team of experts can also help to minimize risks. On your own, it is almost impossible to keep up-to-date with the laws and regulations that may affect your business. Experts may be expensive but not using them can be more expensive. Review your financial strategy with your accountant and banker. Talk to your attorney about liability and tax laws of the various business structures (sole proprietorship, partnership, LLC, S corporation, C corporation, etc.) to determine which is best for your situation. Use your attorney and insurance agent to review contracts and educate your staff on contracts. Review corporate documents and procedures with your attorney. Do not be afraid to pick up the phone to talk with experts and trusted advisers and learn from them. You don't know what you don't know, and a second opinion is always good.

Many of the owners brought up staffing and dealing with employees as one of the most difficult parts of the business. "The more employees you have the greater the risk,"[49] one owner states. He provides an example of an ongoing class action lawsuit initiated by a terminated truck driver claiming he was unable to take the required lunch break due to traffic problems. Several of the owners chose not to have employees due to the difficulties and complexities that they present. One owner discusses the risks of having staff that are not aligned with the company vision and values, and another talks about the importance of trust with your employees. Staffing issues mentioned range from difficulties in hiring and scheduling to theft of company property and employees acting for personal gain at the expense of the company reputation. Several owners minimize risk by knowing every aspect of the business so that they can step into other positions when they have staffing gaps.

Another topic brought up by the owners is the risk or benefit of employees unionizing. Although the likelihood of unions coming into small businesses is low, the risk is real in some industries. Unions can create a loss of control and flexibility for small business owners, and some would rather close their business than be subjected to this.

One owner discusses the stress involved in dealing with the business risks that are out of your control. "You can control only a small percentage of the variables that affect your business, and it's how you take advantage of this percentage that makes the difference," he says.[50]

---

[49]Jacobs (2024).
[50]Johnson (2023).

Effectively managing risks is of primary importance for the continuum of both you and your business. It directly relates to your stress level, happiness, and success in business ownership.

"It takes 20 years to build a reputation and five minutes to ruin it. If you think about that, you'll do things differently."

—Warren Buffett

Owner Feature

Chris Clifton, owner of Southview Design Inc. from 2009 to 2023, led this landscape design–build firm through significant growth with his hard work and strategic, organized approach. His background includes a finance degree, MBA, and a prior business ownership venture. He advises to experience the industry nuances firsthand by working for someone else and then buy an existing business and build it up. When gauging business risk, Chris talks about making "calculated bets" and the need to "believe the odds are sufficiently in your favor." He explains that buying an existing business with an established client base and established cash flow is less risky than starting up a new business. "Pick a business that is somewhat fragmented, meaning it's not impossible to break into … not something that is super concentrated in the hands of a few big, strong players," he says.

Basics to Know About Business Insurance

Business insurance can be customized for your needs and the particular risks for your industry, and it is often bundled together into plan groups. The common types of insurance that are offered include the following:

General Liability—coverage for injury or property damage claims due to you or your employees not using reasonable care.
Product Liability—coverage for injury or property damage claims due to products you or your employees designed, manufactured, or sold.

Professional Liability—coverage for negligent errors and omissions claims due to work that was performed by you or your employees.

Employment Practices Liability—coverage for employment related claims due to inappropriate or unfair acts.

Directors and Officers Liability—coverage for personal claims against directors and officers due to wrongful actions.

Commercial Property—coverage for damage to your building and its contents due to fire, theft, or natural disasters.

Commercial Auto—coverage for injuries and property damage for company-owned vehicles and employee-owned vehicles used for business purposes.

Workers' Compensation—coverage for employee injuries that happened at work.

Cyber Liability—coverage for losses due to cyberattacks or computer incidents.

Business Interruption—coverage for loss of income due to damaged or destroyed property.

Additional details about business insurance can be found through the Insurance Information Institute on their website at www.iii.org.

CHAPTER 8

Rewards

Owning a successful business has countless rewards. For some people the rewards outweigh the effort and commitments required. For others this is not the case.

What is your personal motivation for wanting to own a business? The allure of freedom and money may be the perception of what business ownership can bring, but it is not necessarily reality. Your freedom will be directly related to your goals, customer demands, and support from partners and/or employees. The money you make will be directly tied to the results you achieve. And while you will have power, a humble approach is more effective in leadership roles.

Having a passion for what you are doing, loving a challenge, and being in control of your destination ring true to me as valid reasons for wanting to own a business. Business ownership will take drive, hard work, and persistence. Freedom and money may follow, but having these as your primary motivators is not setting yourself up for success.

Will Business Ownership Provide the Rewards That I Need to Make the Venture Worthwhile?

Am I Motivated by Accomplishments?

The sense of accomplishment that comes with owning and running a successful business can be amazing. This can include providing employment, opportunities, and financial means for others, providing value to customers or communities through needed products or services, or simply meeting your own financial and business goals. There seems to be an endless array of accomplishments to celebrate and motivate you to keep going.

A senior management-level employee told me that our company was the best-run business for which she had ever worked. This one statement provided a huge amount of satisfaction. It was almost too good to be true. I had worked diligently to have the business function like a well-oiled machine, but I had not realized until that moment that I had accomplished this.

Ninety percent of the owners interviewed say that the sense of ownership and pride in accomplishments is one of the primary rewards of business ownership for them. Accomplishments such as bringing their ideas to fruition, seeing positive evidence of their work, bringing value to the world, helping others be successful and bringing their careers along, growing their business, and feeling that their business is a success were all mentions. One owner summarizes this with his statement, "Knowing that I did something that was hard and prevailed."[51]

Do I Enjoy Social Interactions and Notoriety?

As a business owner, new doors will be opened to you such as invitations to events and organizations, the opportunity to meet new people, and the feeling of respect from the community. It can be exciting as well as interesting, offering you a different perspective and understanding of how the world works. You become the face of the company and gain the notoriety associated with it.

Social interaction and notoriety are rewards for many of the owners. The relationships that are developed with customers and business associates, the opening of doors, and professional and customer respect all were named as rewards. One owner talks about waiting on customers and hearing they love your store. "It makes all your time worthwhile," she says.[52]

Am I Willing to Sacrifice Short-Term Gains for Long-Term Financial Rewards?

The financial rewards of business ownership are highly variable and dependent on the financial success of the business. The owners that led their businesses through substantial growth and profits also appear to be

---

[51]Clifton (2023).
[52]Mackenthun (2024).

the owners that took the most substantial financial risks. Typically, you can make more money short term working for someone else, but once the business is established and running smoothly your efforts will be rewarded. You may need to wait until you sell the business to reap the financial payback for your time and hard work. It takes patience.

Financial rewards were mentioned by multiple owners as a secondary benefit and alluded to by others after surviving the initial years. Statements such as, "Creating opportunities for generational wealth for your family," and "Creating wealth for others," support the potential financial rewards of business ownership. But many specifically state they did not do it for the money. Some say the money was better than expected, while others state that they would have been better off financially working for someone else. Several owners talk about getting out of it what you put into it and hopefully being paid back at some point for all those extra hours that you put into the business.

"Entrepreneurship is living a few years of your life like most people won't so you can spend the rest of your life like most people can't."

—Anonymous

Do I Thrive Being My Own Boss?

Being able to set your own direction, challenges, culture and working environment is a reward that many entrepreneurs thrive on. Comments from the owners such as "being in control of my own destiny" emphasize the importance of this. Is the responsibility of being in control of your own destiny something that draws you to business ownership? This is not for everyone; some people need a boss to keep them on track and hold them accountable.

Freedom to do what you want, when you want, on your own terms is a primary reward that was voiced by many of the owners. Multiple statements were made about customizing your job, including doing the work that you love that aligns with your passions and values, having variety in your work, having the ability to hire out everything that you don't love doing, and the flexibility to set your own hours. As an owner, you will have flexibility with your schedule without someone else dictating your when and where, but this will need to be balanced with the needs of the customers and business. The Bob Dylan song "Gotta Serve Somebody" comes to mind—in business your customers become your boss.

"There is only one success—to be able to spend your life in your own way."

—Christopher Morley

Owner Feature

Charlene Roise cofounded Hess, Roise and Company, Inc. in 1990. She transitioned to sole ownership and continued to own the historical consulting firm for 30 years until she sold the business to two of her employees. Charlene says, "It was absolutely worth it!" She talks about the rewards of business ownership in having "a richer sense of the world" and "building a legacy—enabling others to grow and learn, something that is bigger than you." She came from an entrepreneurial family but also credits her business education to books and mentors. She cites optimism, energy, and organization as important traits for business owners. "Love what you are doing and keep fit" she advises. "Corporate jobs are not more stable."

CHAPTER 9

Timing and Exit Strategy

Is This the Right Time for Me to Own a Business?

Do I Have the Knowledge and Experience Needed to Run a Business at This Time?

Industry and management experience is important. Working in a related industry for another small business in a management role or running a branch office for a larger business can provide valuable experience. Can you read and understand a financial statement? And do you have a basic understanding of financial management, accounting, taxes, banking, contracts, insurance, sales and marketing, personal management, benefits, and payroll?

Seventy percent of the owners interviewed did not have a formal business education when they started down the ownership path. Mentors, books, and the school of hard knocks are learning commonalities of the owners. Sixty percent of the owners had parents that owned small businesses, and many said that their parents and the values that they instilled in them contributed to their business success. Learning from past employers, consultants, friends, and others they trust as well as various programs, classes, and seminars are all mentions. Opinions vary as to the value of a business degree for running a small business. The owners that have formal business training agree that a business degree is helpful but not necessary. The owners advise to learn as you go—take every opportunity to advance your education and knowledge base—but experience is key. Learn the ropes of management and your industry by working for someone else before you go into business for yourself.

Is the Opportunity Timely?

Is your idea for a start-up timely? One owner talks about the importance of acting quickly when you see demand for something that is not already being done or provided and is in line with what you love.[53]

Have you identified an existing business that you would like to acquire, or do you have an offer from an existing company to join in as a partner? Do not rush the decision, but don't delay it either. If the stars are aligning right now, go for it. The opportunity may not come again.

Does your family understand and support the commitments that will be needed, and do you have a business mentor or adviser? Are you able to put aside other things right now to make the business a priority? Look closely at your other priorities and commitments. Do you have the energy and stamina to own a business at this time?

Does the Timeline Make Sense with My Exit Strategy?

How many years would you like to own the business? As part of the decision to own a business and the timing of when you own a business, the exit plan should be considered.

The first 10 years of business ownership are exciting and challenging. But what happens after that? Can you keep yourself motivated and inspired? Constant improvement and adaptation to the changing environment are needed to keep a business successful. When you own a business, you can't just say, "I quit" and walk out the door. It can take many years to prepare and execute a successful exit.

Is age a factor that you need to consider? If you are 50 or older, you may want to move forward now if you would like to retire in your 60s. It will take time to make the business yours, whether it is a start-up or an existing business. Ten years is a reasonable time to allow for a business to be running smoothly and when you can start to see the financial rewards.

Would you like to sell the business to an outside party or provide for an internal transition? Will you be prepared to turn over the reins when

---

[53]Patrick (2025).

the time comes? It is difficult to let go of something that you developed and fought for all those years. What if you want to retire but cannot find someone to buy the business? Think through your exit strategy and keep this in mind as you contemplate the timing for your business ownership.

Less than half of the owners interviewed had an exit strategy in mind when they started in business, and most of those strategies changed out of necessity through the years. Some thought they would work forever. Others look back and say they should have sold previously when the economy and business were strong. A struggle with an exit from the business is an apparent commonality for most of those interviewed.

Unrealistic expectations and changes in internal and external circumstances have had a significant effect on the exit plan for many of the owners. Several owners mention the importance of market timing for both selling and buying a business. Making the business scalable and franchising, forming an employee stock ownership plan (ESOP), and forming a perpetual purpose trust are some of the exit strategies that were brought up by the owners for consideration.

The overall advice from the owners is to start working on your exit plan 10 years in advance of when you want to exit and to choose your successor(s) early on, as applicable. It may take several tries to get it right. Multiple owners provided examples of a selected successor that did not work out. The selected successor did not have what it takes. Other owners provided examples of selling to a third party that did not work out. Issues included the buyer not having the required financial qualifications, the buyer not agreeing to requested employment terms, and the partners not aligned on their expectations.

Basics to Know About Selling a Business

Determining the Right Buyer: Employees, customers, competitors, vendors and other complementary businesses, and private equity firms are all potential buyers. Meeting with potential internal and external buyers to find a good fit for your business is a first step. You may want to hire an agent to be proactive in getting your business on the market.

Timeline: Selling a business is a process that takes time and preparation. You will want to take into consideration the following:

- Maximize the value of your business by timing your sale for when your business is on an upswing and the market is good.
- Get your documents in order. Buyers will typically ask for a look back into the company for the last three to five years. This will include financial statements, tax returns, and a list of major customers and sales. A forecast will also typically be requested for upcoming sales including a backlog of work currently under contract and pending proposals.
- Preparation for the sale may need to include training employees to manage the business in your absence, especially if you are planning for an internal transition. Depending on the employees' level of experience, five years is a reasonable length of time to allow for business management and leadership training.
- It is not uncommon for the buyer's terms to require the existing owner(s) to continue employment with the company for up to three years after the sale to ensure a smooth business transition and customer continuance.

Determining fair market value: Prior to going to market with your business, you will need to understand the value of your business. If you do not have an established valuation, you will want to hire an independent appraiser to provide a current valuation of your business.

Types of acquisitions: A stock sale transfers the company stock in a corporation to the buyer, thereby transferring all or a portion of the corporate entity to the buyer. The seller typically prefers a stock sale. It eliminates double taxation for the seller if they are a C corporation and puts more risk on the buyer. An asset sale transfers assets and sometimes liabilities to the buyer. The corporate entity is not transferred. The buyer typically prefers an asset sale. It provides buyer tax advantages and leaves more risk with the seller.

Self-assessment: Do I Have What It Takes to Generate Business Success?

Do I have the key traits that are helpful in running a small business?

Determination and Resilience:
1. Do I have confidence in my ability to succeed and a positive mindset?
2. Am I determined and willing to put in the effort needed?
3. Am I willing to stand up for what I believe in?
4. Can I pick myself up when things go wrong?

Decision Making:
5. Do I have the courage and discipline to make timely decisions that are in the best interests of the business?
6. Do I have sound judgment?

Leadership:
7. Can I inspire and motivate others and myself?
8. Can I convey my big picture ideas and solutions to others?
9. Can I develop a high-performance team and keep them working toward a common goal?

Problem-Solving:
10. Do I enjoy the process of resolving problems and taking responsibility for the solutions?
11. Am I good at investigating, figuring out options, and then extrapolating out the impacts?
12. Can I negotiate to provide the best solutions for the business?

Initiating Action:

13. Can I act quickly to take advantage of opportunities, follow through on decisions, and implement my ideas?
14. Do I have the desire to drive performance or am I more comfortable maintaining the current situation and not ruffling feathers?

Can I apply strategic thinking to the business?

15. Can I organize my thoughts, sorting through the potential opportunities and hurdles, to develop a plan for implementation and long-term growth?
16. Can I align the business goals with my personal goals?
17. Can I think locally, regionally, and globally to forecast changes, needs, and impacts to the business and customers in the next year, in 5 years, and in 10 years?

Do I have a passion for the business?

18. Do I have a passion for the company mission?
19. Do I have a passion for business management?
20. Do I have a passion for the industry?
21. Do I have a passion for the specifics of what I will be doing?

Can I develop and maintain the relationships needed for a successful business?

22. Have I considered business partners?
23. Do I have customer relationships that I can tap into?
24. Do I have a support group?
25. Do I have connections to help me develop a trusted professional network?
26. Do I understand my competitors?
27. Do I have vendor relationships that I can tap into?
28. Can I keep my employees happy and engaged?

Am I willing to make the necessary commitments to run a successful business?

29. How much time do I have to dedicate to the business, and will that amount of time achieve the results that I am after?

30. What other areas of my life require time commitments, and can I create a workable balance?

31. Do I have the money needed for the initial investment in the business?

32. Do I have the financial resources to back a line of credit or loan? And am I comfortable pledging my personal assets for the business?

33. Do I have cash reserves for emergency situations?

Do I understand cash flow?

34. Do I understand what it will take to keep the business in motion?

35. Do I have the discipline to manage the business within a budget?

36. Can I cash flow the initial business investment?

Am I willing to take risks?

37. Can I adapt and change to the outside environment?

38. Can I manage risks to an acceptable level within my inner circle?

Will business ownership provide the rewards that I need to make the venture worthwhile?

39. Am I motivated by accomplishments?

40. Do I enjoy social interactions and notoriety?

41. Am I willing to sacrifice short-term gains for long-term financial rewards?

42. Do I thrive being my own boss?

Is this the right time for me to own a business?

43. Do I have the knowledge and experience needed to run a business at this time?

44. Is the opportunity timely?

45. Does the timeline make sense with my exit strategy?

PART 2

What Is Owning a Business Really Like?

CHAPTER 10

A Day in the Life of an Owner

What is it like to own a business? My business management routine is shared below to provide an example of the day-to-day roles and responsibilities of small business owners. The daily routine and the amount of time needed to manage the business can vary greatly depending on the size and specifics of your business as well as the proficiencies of those around you. You may want to concentrate on your particular area of expertise, but you will need to oversee all aspects of the business. You cannot ignore management of the business if you want to be successful.

If you are starting a business, initially you (and your start-up team) will need to do everything. You will need to do the trade/provide the service/make the product, as well as manage the business. As the business grows the business management time will need to increase. The more employees and customers that you have and the more products and services that you generate, the more time it will take to manage. You may have partners or be able to hire staff to do some of the management, but you will need to fill in the gaps and adjust to the priorities and needs of the business. The daily routine is constantly changing.

While there isn't really a typical day when you are a business owner, here is a business management routine that has worked well for me as the owner and president of a 30-person consulting firm. With one partner, I spent approximately 50 percent of my time on management of the business. We each managed about one-half of the employees and one-half of the operations. When I transitioned to sole ownership, 90 percent of my time was spent on management of the business. My business management time focuses on three major objectives: setting the company direction, managing finances, and managing operations. They all require big picture thinking. This is not about specific tasks but about keeping your thoughts and actions centered on the success of the business as a whole.

Setting Company Direction

Setting the company direction includes internal communications to provide direction and share information, external communications to give myself an outside perspective, and strategic thinking to keep me on track with the business objectives.

Providing employee guidance and answering questions is an important part of my day. Every day I start out with my morning coffee while checking and responding to e-mails and voicemails. This includes weekends and vacation days to catch and address any urgent matters. Sometimes this takes 15 minutes and at other times several hours. Making sure that I am timely with responses is important to keep others moving in the right direction.

Impromptu conversations can consume a large amount of my time. My brain often feels like a pendulum being swung from one area of the business to another. An operations question will follow with an accounting question, then a staffing question followed by a contract question. Most decisions can be made on the spot, but some may require collaboration with others or research that needs to get worked into my schedule. I attempt to put order to the chaos by scheduling weekly check-in meetings with direct reports to stay centered on our business goals. A line of people at my door is a red flag that I need to delegate more or spend additional time in the office available to my staff.

Additional employee time that I fit into my schedule includes orientation sessions for new hires, mentoring sessions for promising younger staff, and meetings with the earmarked future leadership team.

Friday lunches are reserved for meetings with my business partners. The partner meetings are about keeping each other informed and moving in the same direction as well as providing a forum for discussion of ideas and concerns.

My goal is to set up at least one external meeting every week. This includes meetings with customers, consultants or business associates, and networking events. Some of these are in the evenings, and if travel is involved this will increase the needed time allotment. Outside perspectives are important to keep me grounded and informed so that I can make the best decisions for the business.

A block of time on Wednesdays is set aside for research, reading, planning, and strategic thinking. This is valuable time to clear my brain of clutter and do some deep thinking about the business and set priorities and agendas for upcoming meetings. I have found that working from home or somewhere else out of the office is best to get that much needed uninterrupted time for deep thinking. A full day is ideal, but two to four hours a week is usually sufficient to keep me on track with the big picture business goals.

Managing Finances

Managing finances includes monitoring and understanding the current financial position and making the necessary adjustments to meet the financial objectives. I have been fortunate to have an in-house accountant/bookkeeper to manage the day-to-day transactions and prepare the necessary reports for my review. Our year-end financial statements and taxes are outsourced to a Certified Public Accountant (CPA) firm.

Monday mornings are reserved for reviewing data from the previous week, including cash in and cash out. I note abnormalities in expenses and trends in cash flow. Reviewing this information weekly is critical for cash flow decisions.

I spend several days at the beginning of each month reviewing billing and bank statements. This is followed by a mid-month review of the monthly financial statements detailing profit and loss, accounts payable, and accounts receivable. Depending on the state of these items, I may then have a flurry of efforts needed on collection calls, purchasing, or budget cuts to adjust and respond to the data. I have found that getting these statements and reviewing and reacting to them quickly is essential for good financial management.

Occasional meetings with our bank and CPA firm are scheduled as needed.

Managing Operations

Managing operations includes monitoring and understanding the current and upcoming workload and quality control and then adjusting to this information. Managing the operations is a team effort with my department managers. I have not had the luxury of having a lead operations person on staff.

Monday morning data reviews include employee time allocation from the previous week to monitor workload and look for trends such as too many overtime hours or not enough production hours. I supplement this with weekly scheduling meetings focused on scheduling, workflow, quality control, and making go/no go decisions on new project pursuits.

As part of the billing review at the beginning of each month I review project budgets and contract status to look for potential issues and keep updated on project status, which may lead to conversations with staff and customers. Mid-month reviews include work-in-progress and backlog reports. Responding to this information may include an increase or decrease in marketing efforts, initiating hiring or layoffs, or process improvements.

General Time Allocation

What I spend my time on has a big effect on the business results. A routine with some structure is best to keep me focused on the big picture items, but I try not to book more than 50 percent of my weeks to allow adequate time for the day-to-day matters that need to be addressed. Miscellaneous things that come up during the month include new business opportunities, customer concerns, employee concerns, process glitches, contract reviews, staffing issues, and various efforts regarding taxes, insurance, equipment, and benefits. The expertise of my staff at the time determines my level of involvement in each of these.

Special projects are prioritized and fit into my schedule. I have found that the priority, high impact items need to be prescheduled to make sure they get done. Having a prioritized list at my fingertips is important so downtime is not wasted. This can include things like staff training, developing procedures and standards, and website updates.

Complex problems are often sorted out in the evenings, discussing them with my spouse or friends. I let my subconscious work through the options while I sleep which often reveals a clear path in the morning.

CHAPTER 11

Experiences

Some of my experiences and ponderings are provided below to provide insight into what it is like to own a business and share some of the challenges.

Background

I had no dream of owning a business. I did not grow up with parents, friends, or close relatives that owned businesses. My parents, however, both grew up in a small business atmosphere so there is plausibility that some business common sense was indirectly passed down to me through my parents. Business ownership somewhat fell into my lap and it was an opportunity that was too good not to pursue.

I am determined, am a good decision maker, enjoy problem-solving, and like to be proactive. I am not, however, a natural leader. I am an introvert and prefer to be by myself; therefore, the people part of the business has been challenging for me.

An understanding of cash flow is something that I grew up with and is a definite strength of mine. When I was 10 years old my mother taught me to tabulate debits, credits, and cash on hand in conjunction with starting me on an allowance and opening a savings account in my name. I have been managing my cash flow diligently ever since.

Time commitment for my work and career is not something that I had thought about prior to getting involved in business ownership. I came from a family that worked standard 8 to 5 weekday hours along with some occasional Saturday mornings. My parents enjoyed their jobs and were very committed to them, but they did not work extensive hours. I do recall that my dad was called in to work while we were on vacation, but this was an anomaly.

When I started down the ownership path, I was a civil engineer with no formal business training. The only business course I had taken in college was Business Law. Looking back, taking additional business courses to have more basic business knowledge at the beginning would have made life much easier.

The Beginning

I had been employed with my company as an engineer for five years when the company's founders selected me along with a few others to become part of the ownership team. I gradually obtained stock in the company, going from a handful of shares to a 20 percent ownership position over the next 10 years. During these years I was exposed to various areas of the business, but the senior partners took responsibility for the business management.

As the company ownership transitioned and the senior partners left, I deduced that my best options were to either take over running the business or leave. I contemplated the decision for a couple of weeks, discussing it with my spouse and friends. I decided to *go for it* and purchased the additional stock required to give me majority ownership. My decision to stay and lead the company sent me headfirst into the business world.

I started digging into the company files, meeting with staff, and reviewing procedures. I wanted to know everything about how the business was run. When I saw something that I did not like, I implemented changes. I signed up for some one-day classes to provide an overview of accounting and marketing. I found the library to be a great resource, and I checked out books one subject at a time to fill in my knowledge gaps. A friend offered to walk me through putting together a business plan. A whole new world was unfolding.

The year following my purchase of majority ownership, my spouse was presented with an opportunity to join a manufacturing business as a partner. The existing owners were looking for someone to manage the business as they approached retirement. Several years later an opportunity was identified for a new improved product, so my spouse also became part of a new start-up business. We went from a one-business family to a three-business family in a handful of years. It was busy and exciting times and afforded me the opportunity to observe and compare notes with businesses in a different industry.

Relationships

Relationships are something that I had not thought much about prior to business ownership. I generally get along with most people but had not been proactive in reaching out to others. I was the person at school that listened attentively but never raised my hand, waited for my friends to call me, and hated small talk. My determination to have a successful business motivated me to change this. I joined multiple industry organizations, attended networking events, and started reaching out to those individuals that I had met. This started the ball rolling for me bringing in knowledge, industry information, customer referrals, and some great friendships.

Partners

I have had the opportunity to see business partners come and go, and to run the business on my own. Some partners left due to retirement, others for new opportunities or because their business goals did not align with the other partners. We have a shareholder buy–sell agreement in place and developed a valuation formula for the share price to eliminate arguments when partners decide to leave.

As company ownership transitioned over the years, my experience included being part of an ownership team with five, four, and then two principal owners, as well as being the sole principal owner. All these scenarios functioned adequately as the partners had similar core values and respect for one another. I look back now and realize how fortunate I was to have good partners with no major disputes.

I most enjoyed the years with two principal owners and found this scenario to function the best. The partners were in alignment with the business philosophy, business goals, and fiscal management. We respected each other, complemented each other's strengths and weaknesses, and enjoyed our many business discussions over lunch or a glass of wine. I cannot emphasize enough the importance of a good fit with partners.

I observed a not-so-good partner scenario with the start-up business that my spouse was involved with. One of the partners was the technical expert, but his fiscal management and core values did not align with those of the other partners. The beginning years were exciting and fun including world travel to get their new product tested and out to market. But trust between partners eroded rapidly as monies were spent and litigation ensued. Stress started to set in as I noted my spouse had that *green* look. The partners ended up in mediation and terminated their business relationship with bitter emotions that linger to this day.

Customers

I have found that most customers are trustworthy, but some can be ruthless. Here is an example of a ruthless customer.

We landed a big, exciting project and did not do our due diligence in checking on the customer. We were about halfway through the project when I noticed a payment issue. I went to discuss the payment issue with the project manager but found him to be nonresponsive, saying that he had not been feeling well. After some digging, I realized his not feeling well was being caused by the stress of the project. We were deep in the weeds on this one. We underestimated the effort required on the project based on verbal direction from the customer. Now they were not acknowledging out-of-scope work, not paying us, and then proceeded to hire away a handful of our staff. There was no trust in this relationship. We went through a mediation process and learned some hard lessons. We ended up with an enormous amount of unpaid labor on this project before it was closed out. A couple of quick calls to business associates would have told us that this customer had a bad reputation. We have now implemented a go/no go process before pursuing projects including consideration of customer core values and financial history. Knowledge and trust of a customer has proved to be invaluable.

Support Group and Professional Network

My support group throughout my ownership has included current and former business partners, my spouse, and a friend with significant business experience. It took me many years to develop a network of other business owners outside of my immediate circle. Friendships formed with these other business owners have been valuable to me both personally and from a business standpoint.

In addition to accountants and attorneys, my important professional advisers have included both an insurance agent and a banker. Our insurance agent has been a key resource for our business for 40 years providing valuable advice, contract review, and annual training for our staff on topics covering contracts and liability. Our banking seemed like a rotating door for several years as the bankers with whom we had a relationship left the bank. We switched banks and bankers multiple times during my tenure as an owner before finding a good fit. But the result has been finding a banker that has been a valuable resource.

Competitors

I have found competitors to generally be cordial and good to work with, but there have been a couple of instances that remind me to exercise caution when dealing with them.

One day I got a call from a business owner asking if I would like to go to lunch. I was familiar with the company but did not know her. Wanting to be friendly, I agreed. We had a nice lunch discussing the industry, markets, and our businesses. She was assertive, dynamic, and inquisitive. She claimed they had a need for one of our services and asked if we would be willing to help them out. I hesitated. She sensed my hesitation and then dug in with questions. There was a big demand in this service area at the time, and it did not make sense that we would use our current capacity to help a competitor. Several months later I found that she had expanded her business to include this service area in direct competition with us. I then realized that I had shared too much information.

Several years later on a Friday evening I received a call from another business owner. He was desperate for help with a big proposal. We had met for lunch several times so I knew him and wanted to help him out. My company had a good deal of experience in this type of work and we could not pursue this project due to a conflict of interest. So, I spent my Friday evening on the phone with him discussing the proposal. He ended up getting the project and I was happy for him. I thought he would be thankful and return the favor sometime, but I was wrong. He was understaffed to handle the work and proceeded to try to lure away my staff. This was a potential consequence I had not thought through. Needless to say, we no longer go to lunch.

Subconsultants and Vendors

Many of our subconsultants and vendors have been with us for decades and we have developed a level of trust with them. I have one memorable learning experience when venturing out to find a new subconsultant. We had a good customer that asked us to submit a proposal for a project that required expertise that we did not have in-house. After difficulty finding someone to do this work, we contracted with a company that a supplier had recommended without asking a lot of questions. We had not worked with this company in the past and found out the hard way that we were not a good fit. The company did not meet our quality and service standards, was not supportive of our relationship, and attempted to go rogue on us at a customer meeting. We would have been better off not submitting a proposal on this project. The customer held us responsible for the issues and we lost them as a good long-term customer.

My spouse experienced a notable parting of ways with a vendor. The vendor was a big corporation with good quality, pricing, and delivery, but their payment terms were nonnegotiable. Running a small company with limited cash reserves, he needed flexibility in vendor payment terms to match the payment terms of their customers. He opted to go with a smaller vendor that is more expensive but works with them on payment terms.

Employees

I have seen the gamut of employees over the years, and there are a few gold stars that stand out. I wonder what the future would have looked like if the stars had aligned, and all of those gold stars had remained. We have a core group of great employees that have worked together for decades, but it has been challenging finding and keeping people that are top performers outside of that core group.

As a small business, we found ourselves becoming a training ground. We would get people in the door, train them, and then lose them to the bigger salaries and better benefits of larger companies or government agencies. It became important to look for employees who see value in working for a small business and the opportunities that it presents.

Dealing with employees has been the most challenging and frustrating part of the business, but it also has been the most rewarding. I have had emotional staff that would come into my office, shut the door, and start crying. I received e-mails from key staff on weekends stating they were quitting. We have had to deal with fistfights, drug and alcohol problems, depression and anxiety, public complaints about inappropriate behavior, and new employees not showing up. Here are some stories of the good turning bad, the sad, and the ugly.

The Good Turning Bad: We were fortunate to hire a person who had a rare combination of accounting and human resource skills and who also understood business. She developed and documented procedures, supported and trained staff, provided valuable insight and wisdom, and was a great listener. What a joy she was to work with! But when she retired, she left a big gap, and we could not keep up with the systems that she had put in place. Our staff had become comfortable with her level of support, and it took us years to recover. I was surprised at the impact, but we no longer had someone focusing on our employees. This, in turn, seemed to affect morale and undermine trust in our management. We were no longer that great company in our employees' minds without any changes to the business other than losing one staff person.

The Sad: We had another employee who was smart, dedicated, and hard-working. We landed a great project and appointed him to be the field manager on site. The customer liked him as did our staff, and the project was running smoothly. Then we started hearing about parties he was hosting at night, and smelled alcohol on his breath a few mornings. We talked with him about the issue and got some acknowledgment with a promise to do better. A few months later he got picked up for DWI (Driving While Impaired) in our company vehicle. Wanting to do what we could to help him out, we assisted in getting him assigned to a treatment facility for addiction, loaned him some money, and gave him a leave of absence. But he wasn't able to kick the habit, so we had to terminate his employment. He committed suicide a few years later. I felt horrible even though I do not think there is anything more we could have done for him.

The Ugly: We had a senior technical person working on a large three-year project for us who threatened to leave in the middle of the project. We knew that he would be difficult to replace. After several rounds of negotiations, the department manager offered him an increase in pay along with a cash bonus. I was out of the country on vacation at the time, staying connected via e-mail. I did not agree with the decision the department manager was making, but I wanted the manager to take ownership of the situation and I knew that I should support his decision. The manager was the one who knew the employee and his capabilities, and he would have to deal with the difficulties if that employee left. I could foresee that this might affect the morale of the entire department and generate complaints about unfair treatment. It seemed like a short-term solution at the expense of long-term implications. So here I was on vacation by location but not in spirit. I was irritated and it was on my mind for days! Later that year, another one of our senior technical employees in that department ended up leaving, complaining of unfair treatment. The following year, the employee who had negotiated the pay increase and bonus proceeded to leave, taking with him his assistant. We had difficulty hiring replacement staff, causing a third senior technical employee to leave due to overwork. And then the department manager left because he could not deal with the stress of the situation. It was a domino effect stemming from one decision.

Time Commitments

I have found running a small business to be energizing and it can keep me going 24 hours a day if I let it. There are endless possibilities for improvements, marketing and new business development. The research alone can be overwhelming. I seem to have an unquenchable thirst for information and ideas. Business articles and books that held little interest for me previously are now full of applicable information and ideas. There is also a hunger to have conversations and discussions with other like-minded people to discuss ideas and approaches. I enjoy working from home and have not been good at setting boundaries between my work and personal life.

Time off from work has been challenging for me since I took on majority ownership. I have been fortunate to take extended vacations, but to remain responsive and keep the business running smoothly I have felt it necessary to check e-mails daily and address problems from afar. Thus, I don't really get a mental break from work. The flexibility has been great in the fact that I am able to leave the office for weeks at a time, but my mind is only able to take a break from work for short periods of time. My spouse claims that it takes me a week to relax and get work off my mind, and then I start to ramp up with work thoughts again a few days prior to returning to the office. I have not had a backup person that will step up when I am gone and make sure the company as a whole is functioning at an optimum level.

Financial Commitments

The personal financial commitment required for business ownership came as a surprise to me. I had thought that a corporation provided protection for personal finances. When I was in my early years of business ownership I received the following memo from a senior partner:

> Attached are the personal financial and other information required by the SBA and Voyager Bank for the new building. At the time we sign the mortgage each of us will have to guarantee about $1,000,000 personally. Please get these forms back to me by Friday January 22. If you have any questions or need any help let me know. I have more forms if you goof up.[54]

I may have been naive in that I did not have an issue signing the required personal guarantees for the business, but I always had confidence in the fiscal success of the business.

In addition to personal guarantees, my investments in the business included purchasing company stock and providing a down payment for the building. I would not have achieved the financial rewards of

---

[54]Thorp (1999).

business ownership without having the personal finances to support the business needs and the willingness to take on the financial risks of the business with my personal assets.

The Recession

Everything was going extremely well for the first few years until a recession hit and sent us scrambling. Our workload tapered off dramatically leading to discussions about laying off staff and cutting back hours. We ended up doing both. We reduced our staff from 30 to 17 and the remaining staff worked reduced hours. Luckily, we were coming off a good year, and we were able to keep our critical staff throughout the recession.

Several customers stopped paying us. Talking with them revealed that they were having cash flow issues. We started out lenient in our collection process as they had been good paying customers in the past and we trusted they would pay us down the road. We learned the hard way that recession issues hit even the trusted customers. One of them filed for bankruptcy. After a significant amount of effort involving both our attorney and the property owner, we were able to collect half of the amount we were owed.

We had purchased some new vehicles and equipment several years prior with a bank loan. The equipment and vehicles were no longer in use due to our reduced workload, but the payments were still due to the bank. It was not a favorable time to sell—we would most likely have to sell at a loss—so we decided to keep the equipment and vehicles for future needs and figure out a way to maintain the payments.

The owners opted not to take a paycheck to keep the cash flowing to maintain the business. We thought that we would pay ourselves back later, but coming out of a recession is a slow process and there always seemed to be better ways to spend the profits. Our quick reaction and conservative cash flow approach kept the business viable throughout the 2-year recession and ready to take off again when conditions improved.

As the recession was winding down, we received a letter from the bank. A representative version of this letter follows:

This letter serves as written notice that the bank will not automatically renew your line of credit per the terms of the note. While the bank is considering an alternative loan structure, federal regulations require this written response. You have the right to a written statement of the specific reasons for the non-renewal. To obtain the statement, please contact the undersigned representative within 60 days from the date you are notified of our decision. We will send you a written statement of reasons for the non-renewal within 30 days of receiving your request for the statement.

This was disheartening after all we had done to maintain our cash flow. This letter was from the bank's corporate office and could prove to be fatal to the business. Fortunately, we had developed a trusted relationship with our local banker and she worked to get our credit line renewal through the necessary approvals.

Some of our competitors were not so fortunate during the recession. Some lost their businesses and others mortgaged their homes and cashed out retirement accounts to stay afloat.

My spouse and I loaned our businesses money during this tough financial time. We set up loans with interest at the current prime rates. Being in a personal financial position to loan the businesses money was a win-win scenario for both the businesses and for us personally.

Cash Flow

Being diligent with cash flow management has kept the business in a strong financial position throughout the years. Timely review of financial information, annual budgeting, staying on top of workflow, and diligence in collections have all been an essential part of our financial success. We have gradually improved our processes and decision making over the years. Some important lessons that we have learned are as follows:

- Take time to be thorough in your pricing and scope of work, including discussing it with the customer and having a second person review it prior to finalizing.
- Understand your costs and the risks involved, including items like management, transportation, insurance, training, equipment, and inflation.

- Changes in scope of work or other customer direction needs written authorization/documentation prior to doing the work.
- Customers requesting extended payment terms should be a red flag unless you understand and agree with the need and risks involved.
- Those who are most diligent in their collection process tend to be paid first.
- Customers may have a close-out date on projects after which monies may not be available to pay invoices.
- Matching equipment loan terms with the duration for specific project needs saves on future cash crunches.
- Delays in preparing a balanced budget can result in spending money that you don't have.

Managing Risks

I have never considered myself a risk taker, yet I have found that risks are what make business exciting. Knowing how to manage those risks is what takes away the fear and makes it interesting.

One experience that I recall involved working on three different projects for a new customer and having trouble collecting on our invoices. We continued working on the projects for several months in good faith that the customer would pay, but to no avail. After our inquiry, the customer admitted that the person who signed our agreements was not authorized to do so and told us they did not intend to pay us. We went to small claims court in hopes of collecting what they owed us. The judge asked why we continued working for the customer when they did not pay us after 30 days per the agreement. The judge voiced his opinion that we should have known better and that the claim would have been substantially lower if we had done this. I was embarrassed.

This was a wake-up call for me. We started a routine collection process after this that has served us well for many years. The judge did rule in our favor, but we never did get paid for the work due to the customer's lack of funds.

Here is another experience that happened to me—leaving me wishing that I had consulted the experts during our initial strategic planning process. One of my primary goals for the business has always been fiscal strength. I set my mind to eliminating debt as a priority. I did not want our decisions to be controlled by the banks. After our debts were paid off, we opened a savings account to be our own banker, so to speak. Our hope was that we could cover seasonal cash fluctuations, equipment and vehicle purchases, and some of the stock payouts for retiring partners without borrowing money from the bank.

This went on for several years before our CPA consultant questioned this cash asset. They informed us that there could be a potential federal tax on accumulated earnings. I was in shock. This was a taxation I did not know existed, and it affected my entire philosophy of fiscal management for the business. The tax, although seldom enforced, could be substantial and posed a significant risk to the business. Nevertheless, we adjusted our fiscal philosophy limiting our accumulation of cash.

Here are two additional examples of risks. They were circumstances that came from the outside world, were out of our control, and had a significant impact on our business.

I had just taken over as majority owner of the business and we had the opportunity to work on our first big state project. The entire staff was excited, poring over the plans, preparing estimates, and talking to contractors. We had been in business for 25 years at this point and knew the industry well, but we were not familiar with the added level of regulations on this type of project. I read the contract thoroughly and looked up referenced statutes and codes to make sure we knew what was required. The project went well until the end when we received a letter stating that our field people were to be paid a specific prevailing wage rate.

I was in disbelief. We were a professional services firm, and this didn't make sense to me. I thought that this must be a mistake. Our wages exceeded the minimum wage requirements and were competitive with other firms in the area. There was nothing in the contract that indicated our services fell under any specific prevailing wage requirements. We had never been required to pay a given prevailing wage rate in the history of the company, and there was no established wage rate for our services. I discussed this with our attorney and was told that we were exempt from prevailing wage requirements under the Federal law.

It was bad timing, as there was a movement within one department at the State to try to establish prevailing wages for all fieldwork under the contractor for this type of project. After several phone calls to other professional service firms in our industry, I confirmed that this was new territory for everyone, and we were caught in the middle. We had no choice but to fight. The financial impact of these increased wages would most likely put us out of business. We got stuck in a time-consuming 3½-year battle debating this through an administrative hearing process. "Brain Damage" on Pink Floyd's *The Dark Side of the Moon* album got me through many nights during this debacle.

We ended up paying a significant amount in attorney fees, but we did prevail in the end. I learned a lot and actually enjoyed the process and challenge. The moral of the story is that written contracts really do mean something, but it takes a good attorney and considerable time and funds to fight. It was an extremely interesting and frustrating few years.

A second example of a risk that was out of our control involved a government shutdown. We were working on several government projects when the State government shut down work on these projects due to a budget stalemate. It was July, which is the peak of our busy season when we need to make money to cover our slower winter months. We did not know how long this shutdown would last so we did not want to lay off staff. We had a substantial financial loss that July and one employee left to work for a competitor that was not working on government projects, so not experiencing the shutdown. We were asked to submit costs and expenses due to the shutdown, but as a subcontractor we did not qualify for reimbursement of our losses. This was a risk I had not previously considered and there was little I could do about it other than understand that this is a risk we take on government-funded projects.

Rewards

For me, the rewards of business ownership have been plentiful. I am energized by the day-to-day challenges and decision making. I get great satisfaction in helping employees learn and grow in their careers. I am motivated by accomplishments, and I enjoy setting business goals and then seeing them through to fruition.

The opportunities for social interaction and meeting people that business ownership has brought have been incredible. This is not something that motivates me but has been an unexpected benefit. Business ownership has provided a platform for connecting to others resulting in valuable long-term friendships with like-minded people.

Great personal wealth has never been a goal of mine. However, getting the business into a strong and stable financial position has been one of my primary business goals. Setting aside personal financial rewards for the good of the business was not difficult for me. Knowing that my investments in the business were long term and that they would come to fruition, I did not find it difficult to stand on the sidelines as friends and colleagues were buying new houses. I had family members that had better benefits and retirement plans working for large corporations or the government. At one point I was offered double my salary to go work for another company. But the philosophy of delayed gratification worked for me. Investing in a successful business has provided long-term financial rewards that would have been difficult to achieve as an employee.

The idea of being my own boss does not motivate me, yet the freedom and independence to make my own decisions is important to me. I need to be a part of something that I believe in, and business ownership has provided this. Schedule flexibility has been a benefit to me, although not a primary motivating factor. I have been able to travel abroad for three weeks at times, with the caveat of daily check-ins, and I also worked remotely one day a week before this was a common trend.

When I look back, I am glad I have had the opportunity to experience business ownership. It has been exciting, and the learning has been immense. Although I could have made more money in the short term as an employee for someone else, long term my efforts have been rewarded. The people I have met through the years and the relationships that have developed with like-minded business owners are amazing. Doors have opened into another world. I have no regrets.

Exit Strategy

I went into majority ownership thinking I would lead the company for five years and then move on. What I did not think through at the time was how this would play out financially and how this would work with the business partners that were older than me. The five-year mark came and went. We were in a deep recession, not taking salaries and financially unable to consider an exit at this point. Besides that, the recession presented a challenge that I was up to. I was not ready to leave at this point. As we came out of the recession, work picked up and we started to discuss the timing of the partners leaving from a financial standpoint. It made sense that the older partners would exit first and get paid out prior to me leaving. So, I would have to wait.

The next hurdle was who will lead the company after I leave. All the senior management level people would be leaving prior to or at the same time as me. My focus shifted to the following questions: Do I have younger staff that can move up into leadership positions? Are they interested? And do they have the necessary knowledge and traits? Other options for my exit included selling to an outside party and hiring a top-level person to run the business. The company legacy had been to promote from within and to offer company stock to key staff and this was my preferred path. I wanted to provide the same opportunities for my staff as had been provided to me.

We identified multiple bright and dedicated employees for potential leadership roles. None of them had business training or experience and we wanted to get them into leadership roles quickly. I looked outward for help and put a person on our board of directors that had leadership expertise to help guide me through the leadership training and transition. I learned that management things that come naturally to me do not necessarily come naturally to others. We initiated monthly training sessions with these key employees and also developed a leadership ladder and assessment to use throughout the company. The transition process was very time-consuming. It was a five-year process with a lot of ups and downs. Some have not been able to make the transitions required to move up the leadership ladder, others have lacked interest, commitment, or confidence. The transition process resulted in losing some top staff that left big holes in our business. The leadership mindset is extremely important and seemingly rare.

I thought it would be better to phase my exit over several years. This phased strategy seemed like it would be easier on the future leaders, the employees, and myself, allowing for transition time and gradual adjustments. This approach did work, but it proved to be tricky and frustrating. Cutting my hours back and not giving the business my complete attention was a struggle for me. It is difficult to let go of something that you have built and nurtured for 40 years.

CHAPTER 12

Q and A

Many questions have been posed to me over the years about business ownership. Some of these have come from training sessions with future ownership teams, others from those with a mild curiosity about ownership and what it entails. Here are the questions posed and responses.

How Do You Know What Needs to Be Done?

Experience, common sense, and intuition play a significant role in knowing what to do when you are running a business, but educating yourself is also important. Basic knowledge in finance, marketing, business law, and human resources is critical in understanding your options, the impacts of your decisions and what actions are needed.

Knowledge in accounting, taxes, and banking as well as cash flow and budgeting will assist in your financial management. An understanding of marketing and business development will help you identify needs to grow the business. Knowledge of pertinent laws, contracts, and insurance will assist in keeping your business moving along without major setbacks. If you have employees, basic knowledge and an understanding of the processes involved in payroll, hiring, firing, training, and benefits will assist you with your human resource management and keep you out of trouble.

This may seem overwhelming if you do not have experience in these areas, but some reading and/or taking a business class in these topics will go a long way. You do not need to be an expert in these areas, but you do need to know enough to ask the right questions, know when you need to consult with the experts, and then know enough to oversee the experts and run their advice through your own filter and be able to apply it.

How Do You Know if Something Slips Through the Cracks?

The reality of business is that some things will slip through the cracks. You can look at minor slips as learning opportunities and respond by implementing improvements to your operations to prevent this from happening again. However, you need to be proactive to make sure that major things do not slip through the cracks.

Developing processes and metrics, and then a schedule for monitoring them will provide early warning signs when things are going astray. This includes everything from financial management to project management. Trust others to do their job but you need to oversee these affairs with steady and careful monitoring. Timely monitoring is crucial to avoid things slipping through the cracks.

In addition to weekly and monthly data review, I set up a calendar for miscellaneous things to monitor such as tax payments and website updates. It is also helpful to have a list of high-level questions to periodically review such as: Are the customers happy? Are the employees happy? Are contract requirements being met? Are we managing within our budget? Does our staff count balance with the future workload? Are vendor payments timely? Are quality control processes being followed? Which customers are behind in payment and why?

What Do You Do if You Run Out of Money?

Unfortunately, cash crunches do happen in business. When this occurs, I immediately stop spending on everything except critical items and then dig in to figure out why this is happening. The worst thing you can do is to ignore the situation and just hope that it resolves itself.

Review your accounts receivable. Is there a customer who is not paying your invoices? If so, contact them to find out why they are not paying and when you can expect payment. It may be as simple as they didn't get your invoice, but the situation could be more critical such as they are having cash flow difficulties, or they are not happy with your work. If the customer is nonresponsive, you can send a letter or show up in-person at their office. You will want to review your contract with them to understand your options.

Review your budget and cash flow projections. Are they accurate and is this just a temporary situation? Can you make adjustments or is this a potentially fatal situation?

If this is a temporary situation, talk to your banker and vendors to explain your cash situation. The bank may be able to provide a line of credit, or an increased line of credit to cover your short-term cash needs. Your vendors may be able to extend your payment terms. Communication goes a long way in keeping all those involved on good terms. As a last resort, you can use personal cash reserves and/or put your own salary on hold to get through a short-term cash crunch. Talk to your attorney about options if the financial difficulties appear to be long term and could be fatal.

Proactively monitoring your cash flow and accounts receivable will help you predict and be prepared for cash crunches. The best time to talk to your banker about a line of credit is before you need it. You can negotiate favorable payment terms with your customers and vendors when you are working out the contracts. Favorable payment terms with your customers can include paying for materials upfront, the right to stop working upon nonpayment, and interest charges for overdue payments. Favorable payment terms with vendors can include pay when paid terms.

How Do You Identify the Priorities and Greatest Needs for the Business?

Focusing on the big picture is key for me to identify the priorities for the business. Develop a business plan and use it to guide your decisions. Setting aside blocks of time for deep thinking has been invaluable for me to accomplish this. It is very easy to get involved with the day-to-day details and not to take the necessary time to step back and look at the big picture.

Not all business needs will be clear and direct. Setting priorities often is a balancing act centered on achieving an overall goal. Too much focus in one area can lead to consequences in other areas. Too much training time may lead to a reduction in productivity, while too little training may lead to inadequate quality or poor morale. Understanding the connections and impacts of your actions is important.

Collect and review your company data so that you understand where you are. Monthly review of your balance sheet, profit and loss statements, and backlog is insightful. Then you can adjust, adapt, set priorities, and make informed decisions. If your backlog is down, you may need to spend more time on sales and marketing. If your backlog is up, you may need to focus on hiring.

"The main thing is to keep the main thing the main thing."
—Stephen Covey

What and How Do You Delegate So That You Have Time for Business Management?

How much you can delegate will depend on the size of your business. A larger business requires more business management time and therefore requires more delegation and will have more employees to delegate to. My recommendation is to delegate any task that you can train someone else to do. When something comes up, think more about *who can do this* instead of *what needs to be done*. Is it a definable task and can the needed results be clearly communicated?

Delegation should involve a stepped process of training, observing, and then checking. Understand that both you and your employees are always learning. Once you have confidence in their abilities, give them the authority to make decisions and hold them accountable, but maintain some degree of oversight. Define critical items that need your approval and things that need to be brought to your attention immediately. This process takes time, patience, faith, and trust.

I have found that time management is a critical part of successful business management. Learning to say no to items that others can do is helpful in reserving the needed time for business management. This takes discipline, especially if these items are things that you like to do and are within your comfort zone. Ask yourself, *What should I spend my time on that will provide the most impact to the business?* and then make sure these items are in your schedule. Setting the direction for the business as well as monitoring and oversight are important to include in your schedule. Other items should be delegated so that you have time for the high impact items.

> "The Eye of a Master will do more Work than both his Hands."
> —Benjamin Franklin

How Do You Align the Business with Your Personal Goals and Values?

Putting together a written business plan and owners' plan that are coordinated with each other can ensure that your personal goals and values are reflected in the business. These documents then become an important guideline and tool for managing the business and making decisions.

The business plan can include core values for the business that align with your personal values, and profit goals that align with your personal financial goals. For example, core business values of honesty and integrity can be documented in the business plan and then used as a guideline for business decisions, and the profit goal in the business plan can designate a percentage to be reinvested in the business and a percentage for owner distributions.

An owners' plan documents what the owner(s) personally want out of the business. This plan can include expectations such as salaries, distributions, benefits, working hours, and retirement dates. This document is especially important if you have partners so that each owner's expectations are shared and understood.

What Mindset Shift Is Necessary to Go from a Worker to an Owner?

The extent of the required mindset shift will be dependent on your current role, the size of your current company, and the size of your new business. The mindset shift includes both managing people and managing the business. These mindset shifts are explained in detail in *The Leadership Pipeline*,[55] with modifications needed for small businesses.

If you do not currently manage people, you will need to shift your mindset to getting things done through others. This will require you to understand the importance of your management contributions rather than your individual task contributions. You will need the ability to select and develop employees, negotiate their needs and concerns, allocate resources, and apply strategies. Achieving this mindset means understanding the value of others and setting aside time to train, coach, and oversee them.

Business management requires a mindset shift centered on the business as a whole and your goals for the business. If you are coming from a large corporation this will be a significant change. You will need to adopt a long-term vision and have the ability to set direction and drive performance, manage and integrate your operations, balance the needs of all areas of the business, and proactively make changes. Achieving this mindset means keeping a broad perspective, adjusting to internal and external issues, thinking through short-term and long-term ramifications, and making tough decisions. Self-interests need to be set aside for the good of the company. You will need to understand that managing the business is your most important role and that you need to dedicate the necessary time for it.

What Are the Daily Positives of Owning a Business?

Working toward something that you believe in and setting your own priorities are two major daily positives of owning a business. You make the decisions and take responsibility for the results. You decide how you spend your time, what you want to work on, whom you want to work with, and what hours you work. If things don't turn out, the only one to blame is you. You are in control of your own destiny. You have a sense of freedom and you can express yourself without fear of repercussions, but there will be parameters and constraints from your customers, employees,

---

[55]Charan et al. (2011), 16–30.

and vendors. You may need to adjust your hours and do things that you do not like to accomplish your goals, but this will be your decision.

What Are the Daily Negatives or Issues That May Cause Stress and How Do You Deal with These?

As the owner, you will need to address the daily questions and problems that surface. Some will find this fun and engaging and others will find it stressful. The issues can be as difficult as not having the cash to meet payroll, not having enough work to keep your employees busy, or dealing with irate customers and lawsuits. Emergency situations may need to be addressed at night or on weekends causing additional stress from the expectations of family and friends. Stress motivators are different for everyone. Doing what you do not like or are not good at will likely create stress. Several owners that I know find the sales and marketing part of the business the most stressful because this is out of their comfort range. Others have had to teach themselves to set up spreadsheets for budgeting and tracking expenses when they are not a numbers person.

Getting enough sleep, exercise, a healthy diet, and quiet time for thinking are all key for me in managing stress—and, most importantly, having someone to talk with about business issues. Being able to bounce ideas and concerns off another knowledgeable person and having moral support and understanding from others is a huge stress reliever.

What Is Your Work–Life Balance and Does It Change over Time?

Several owners that I have talked with say that there is no work–life balance, especially for the first 5 to 10 years of owning a business. It depends on your ambitions. For me it is self-inflicted *thinking* time that bleeds into my personal life. I am fortunate to have an understanding and supportive spouse. The divorce rate for the business owners that I interviewed was not higher than the national average. Within my interview group, two of three husband–wife teams that went into business together ended in divorce.

The amount of time needed to own and manage a business can change over time. The initial years of business ownership often take the biggest time commitment. If you are a start-up business you will need to get systems set up, staff hired and trained, and customers in the door. If you are taking over an existing business, you will want to review operations and procedures and make adjustments, talk with staff and customers, and review contracts to get up to speed.

The years prior to your exit of the business can also take an extra commitment of time. Succession planning for internal transitions, including finding the right successor(s) and getting them trained, can be very time-consuming. Sale of your business to an outside party may require hiring an agent, meetings and communications with potential buyers and attorneys, and compiling information and reviewing agreements, all of which are time-consuming.

The necessary time commitment in the middle years of business ownership will vary depending on your growth strategies and your internal and outside environments. Generally, once you have your systems running smoothly and you can call them your own, the time commitment should not be as great. However, things will always come up that will need your time, no matter where you are in your tenure of ownership. Businesses don't stand still—they need constant adaptation.

Do the Key Elements for Owning and Running a Business Change Based on the Industry and Business Size?

I was surprised, after interviewing 16 business owners in different industries and of various sizes, that there were very few differences in responses about *what it takes to generate success.* The industries all need the same basic governance. The size of the business does, however, have a significant effect on the responsibilities of the owners.

If the business does not have employees, the management requirements of the owners are significantly less. Several of the owners interviewed can attest to this as they have decided not to have employees. With micro businesses the owners must take on all the responsibilities and do everything themselves with the assistance of consultants or independent contractors.

As the company grows, the owners can eliminate responsibilities slowly but will still need to oversee all functions. When the company can afford to hire overhead personnel and management staff, the owners can decide what they do and don't want to do, giving them the ability to write their own job description to some extent. Bookkeeping, payroll, benefits administration, and clerical/office management support are often the first responsibilities that owners want to hand off to others.

PART 3

Is Business Ownership for You?

CHAPTER 13

The Decision

The decision to become a business owner is not black and white. There are varying degrees of commitments, risks, and rewards depending on your personal goals and your goals for the business. A one-person business will not take the same level of commitment and risk-taking as growing a business to have hundreds of employees. And slow, steady growth will require a different level of commitment and risk-taking than aggressive growth.

The more knowledge, experience, and relationships that you have the easier it will be for you to hit the ground running. If you don't have experience in business, management, and the industry you will need time to figure it out. You will need to allow for mistakes and setbacks, and attaining success may take longer.

There are also personality traits that make business ownership a better fit for some versus others. While you can learn and adapt as you go, traits tend to be innate and take significant effort to change.

Do I Have What It Takes?

What does it take to generate business success? Part 1 of this book provides questions to contemplate about key elements and considerations for small business ownership. If you can answer *yes* to all these questions, you are well suited to business ownership and have a favorable chance of leading your business to success. If you cannot respond with a *yes* to all these questions, all is not lost. Very few people have all the traits and other key elements mentioned in this book. It is how you address these missing elements that will make the difference.

If you skipped some topics in this book because they did not interest you, you may avoid dealing with these things in your business also. We tend to do what we enjoy and are good at and defer what we do not enjoy or are difficult for us. How will you manage those areas of the business that you do not enjoy or are difficult for you? You will want to dig deeper into these areas to identify the needs for your specific business goals and fill in the gaps to cover your weaknesses.

Understanding your missing elements and gaps, and thinking through what you will do about them is an initial step in the decision-making process. Will you learn as you go by reading, taking classes, and using mentors and advisers; will you hire key employees, and/or find a partner to cover these areas?

Do the Responsibilities and Challenges of Business Ownership Interest Me?

A second step in the decision-making process is to understand where your interests and aptitudes lie. Are you good at doing tasks, or managing people and processes? Do you enjoy working with set parameters, or do you prefer thinking, learning, and adapting? Part 2 of this book provides examples and answers questions about what it is like to own a business. Business ownership is about managing, thinking, learning, and adapting. Do the responsibilities and experiences of business ownership interest you? Will you find joy in the journey and the challenges that business ownership brings?

What is your reason for wanting to own a business? Make sure that you really have the interest and desire to own a business and that this is not just a potential solution to a problem or the path of least resistance. Being unhappy with your current job and looking for a change, or feeling you would be better off being your own boss because you do not take direction well, does not validate your desire for business ownership. Closely think through why you want to own a business and what your big picture objectives are.

Reasons for Failures

Every situation is different, and business ownership is not for everyone. According to the U.S. Small Business Administration, from 1994 to 2020, the five-year survival rate was 48.9 percent for new small businesses with paid employees, and the 10-year survival rate was only 33.7 percent.[56]

---

[56]"Frequently Asked Questions about Small Business" (2023).

Some people decide that business ownership is not for them after a year or two and want to get out. Others hang on too long with a false hope that things will get better. The statistics for small businesses that don't survive the initial few years are staggering. You do not want to be one of those statistics.

Business failure is ultimately tied to lack of cash; you do not generate enough cash to pay the bills. But why this happens is the deeper question. I was given a lengthy list of failure factors in my early years of business ownership. The majority of these failure factors can be grouped into a few general categories: inability of management, poor financial management, and poor relationships. Steve Taplin provides a countering group of failure factors in his article "Decoding Small Business Failures: Top Four Contributing Factors" which include underestimating sales and marketing, inadequate preparation, insufficient effort, and lack of knowledge.[57] Interviews with the owners revealed some additional reasons for business failures: not having a viable business and thinking through what is needed from the start, financial misappropriations, poor inventory management, overly aggressive growth, overconfidence, not understanding themselves, not asking for help when needed, not keeping up with changes, and dysfunctional ownership.

These reasons for business failures are not provided to scare you but as a reality check. Small failures can be overcome and you learn from every one, but you do not want them to become catastrophic.

"Even a mistake may turn out to be the one thing necessary to a worthwhile achievement."

—Henry Ford

What Are the Options for Level of Ownership?

There are several levels of ownership to consider as part of your decision-making process. Would you like to own 100 percent of the business and take this pursuit on alone or is 51 percent or 30 percent ownership

---

[57]Taplin (2024).

an option? The decision to have partners in business is often overlooked and not vetted out as a choice. If the idea of starting or acquiring a business stems from conversations with friends or coworkers, you may simply move forward with them as partners without giving it much thought. If you have been alone in your contemplation of business ownership, you may move forward on your own without exploring other options. I am an advocate of giving partnerships almost as much thought as business ownership. Partners can make or break the business and have a significant effect on whether your experience as a business owner is positive or negative.

Do you need business partners? Experienced partners can be tremendous assets. They can help guide you through the first few years, provide financial capacity, and share in the responsibilities. If you answered *no* to some of the questions in this book, you may want to consider partners. What are your weaknesses or things that you do not like to do? Finding the right partner(s) that complements you and your abilities will be important. If you would like to spread out the responsibilities and financial commitments, you may want multiple partners. But keep in mind that the more partners you have, the more opinions there will be, and the less control you will have over the business.

Equal ownership among partners is not advised to avoid an owners' voting deadlock. One owner warns against a 50:50 percent ownership split as he discusses the issues with decision making. "You can't solve things without lawyers,"[58] he says.

If you can answer *yes* to all the questions in this book, you are a suitable candidate for sole ownership. You get to make the decisions, take responsibility for your actions, and reap the rewards. But you may want business partners even if you don't need them. A collaborative approach may be more appealing to you, or if you have limited business management experience and knowledge, you may want to ease into ownership by working with an experienced partner. Make sure that the benefits of having partners outweigh the negatives. Can you work with them, stay open-minded, understand their strengths, and appreciate their contributions?

---

[58]Patrick (2025).

What Are the Opportunities and Realities?

Have I Identified an Opportunity for a Start-Up Business?

Do you have a unique idea for a product or service that you would like to implement? Is it something that does not currently exist and is there demand for it? Is there a pull to this business that is a result of where life has taken you? And does it align with what you love doing?

New businesses provide the opportunity of a clean slate allowing for creativity and setting up the company exactly as you wish. They can be fun and exciting with the potential for a huge upside. They are also unproven ventures that pose risks of the unknown. Innovation and risk tolerance as well as experience and organization will be key to successful planning and implementation of a start-up business.

You will want to use your connections to figure out the needs of the business. Think through not only if you have a viable business but also if you are willing to make the required time and financial commitments and take the required risks to get this business started. Do you have the time and energy that will be needed and the passion to see it through? You may need to hire and train employees; buy equipment, software, inventory, and supplies; lease or buy a building; purchase insurance; set up banking; set up accounting and payroll systems; develop processes; create a website and other marketing materials; and develop a network of customers, vendors, and consultants. Do you have a start-up team or family and friends that can provide labor and moral support to help you out?

The financial needs for a new business include the capital expenditures for your initial investment as well as the money necessary to cover the lag time until you can get to a point of positive cash flow. You also need to cover your personal expenses until you can pay yourself a salary. Do you have the money to invest in the business and cover your personal expenses, or do you have family members that can provide financial support? A start-up business loan is the most difficult type of funding to get. If you find a bank to provide funding for your start-up, they will expect the owner(s) to provide a substantial down payment (25 to 30 percent) on the necessary investment.

Have I Identified an Existing Business That I Am Interested in Acquiring?

Do you have experience in this or a similar industry? Do you have experience working in a comparable size business? Does the business resonate with you? Do you have ideas for improvement or expansion?

Acquiring an existing business may pose less risk than a start-up if you do your homework. It has established processes, employees, customers, consultants, vendors and an existing cash flow. Due diligence is critical to fully understand what you are buying and what you are getting into. Ask many questions and talk with the frontline workers to get an inside perspective. Talk with others within the industry to get an outside perspective. You will need to be ready to deal with the baggage that comes with existing businesses. This could include problem employees, a less than stellar reputation, difficult customers, and poor processes. Old habits are difficult to change, and they take time to change. You will need to be a strong leader to implement and enforce changes and be good at problem-solving. Building a good management team that is aligned with your business goals will also be important and key to growing the business and putting your stamp on the business.

Acquiring an existing business requires a substantial financial investment. This could be seller financed, or bank financed, with variable terms depending on the buyer's reputation and financial status. The purchase price along with monies for capital improvements will need to be included in the financing. Do you have the money for a down payment on the loan? And can you cash flow the principal and interest payments of the loan? A careful analysis of the cash flow will be needed.

Have I Been Asked to Join an Existing Business?

If you are asked to join an existing business as one of the principal owners, this is a wonderful opportunity to learn about business under the guidance of existing partners. Experience becomes less important. If this is a business where you currently work, it is a known commodity, but due diligence will still be critical so that you know what you are getting into. You will want to pay attention to who has controlling interest for decision making and who are the influencers. The existing partners will have established their relationships, methods, and ideas, so you will need to use your leadership and negotiating skills to get changes made. Reviewing the existing business plan and ownership agreements will be important. Accept that it may be difficult to make changes.

Your initial investment will most likely be lower than acquiring an entire business, but you will have less control, and you may need to wait until you sell the business to see a return on your investment. Understand that your financial risk is tied to the personal financial portfolio of your partners. In the case of a default on a business loan, the bank will not distribute the obligations among the partners; they will go after the most easily obtained assets. If you have the accessible assets, you could be on the hook for the entire loan amount.

Do I Have an Opportunity to Take Over the Family Business?

The legacy of a family business is appealing to many. You may be in a position to take over the business from a parent and/or provide an opportunity for your children to continue in the family business. You may want to work with your brothers, sisters, a spouse, or other relatives to keep the business all in the family. The same questions should be asked with a family business as with any other business, and the same due diligence should be completed to make sure you know what you are getting into. You may have come up through the ranks working in the business, but does the business resonate with you? Do you have ideas for improvement or expansion? Try to take the emotions out of the decision.

The financial aspect of ownership in a family business can be a big positive. Initial investment could be minimal, or family-backed financing could be provided.

Family businesses can be complex and present unique issues that warrant special owners' plans to assure that all parties are in agreement. Children may not want to work in the family business even though this is the expectation. Or they may feel entitled to ownership even if they have not been selected as a successor. It is also possible they will feel guilty about getting the business handed to them. Disagreements between family members can get emotional and cause rifts throughout the family.

Preferential treatment of family members can be an issue with other employees. The opposite can also occur where family members expect more from each other, potentially leading to bad feelings. Objectivity can be lost and relationships within the family can be damaged.

Is Small Business Ownership for Me?

Becoming a small business owner is a life-changing decision. Take time to think through the topics in this book so that you can work your way through this decision with your eyes open. You don't need to know everything at the start, but it is helpful to understand what it will take and what it is like. Most of the business owners that were interviewed found success by figuring it out as they went along and by taking advantage of the experience of others through mentors and peers. You may want to talk with other business owners in your industry to understand the realities of what it will take before you take the plunge.

Look at the business ownership decision from a big picture perspective. Business can be fulfilling and fun if you are a good fit for the challenges and your interests and goals align. Positive vibes were received from over 90 percent of the owners about their business ownership experience. Looking back, you tend to remember the big picture positives of business ownership and forget the small frustrations and hard work. You do need to step up and put in the required effort for the business to survive, but hopefully it all becomes worthwhile if you achieve your objectives—whether it is the independent lifestyle, excitement of the day-to-day challenges, or your big picture mission.

Small business ownership can be extremely rewarding and plays an important part in our society. One owner conveys this well with his statement, "We need to encourage people to have initiative and to be independent, and to work under the stars at the end of the day. We do, or else we lose that edge."[59]

---

[59]Rehkamp (2025).

References

Balke, Lisa Clark (Owner, Victory Vintage LLC, www.shopvictory.com, 2015–Present). Face-to-Face Interview with Author, December 4, 2023.

Belin, Sandra (Owner, Jacobs Farm/Del Cabo, Inc., www.jacobsfarmdelcabo.com, 1980–Present). Face-to-Face Interview with Author, December 8, 2024.

Charan, Ram, Steve Drotter, and Jim Noel. 2011. *The Leadership Pipeline*. 2nd ed. Jossey-Bass.

Clifton, Chris (Owner, Southview Design Inc., www.southviewdesign.com, 2009–2023). Virtual Interview with Author, December 6, 2023.

Ellis, Charles D. 2013. *What It Takes: Seven Secrets of Success from the World's Greatest Professional Firms*. John Wiley & Sons.

Farr, Edward (Owner, Edward Farr Architects, Inc., www.edfarrarch.com, 1991–Present). Face-to-Face Interview with Author, January 4, 2024.

"Frequently Asked Questions About Small Business." 2023. U.S. Small Business Administration; Office of Advocacy. https://advocacy.sba.gov/wp-content/uploads/2023/03/Frequently-Asked-Questions-About-Small-Business-March-2023-508c.pdf.

Hanson, Mike (Owner, Hunt Electric Corporation, www.huntelec.com, 1996–2021). Face-to-Face Interview with Author, January 14, 2025.

Hartman-Wrolson, Debby (Owner, St. Boni Bistro LLC, 2017–2023). Face-to-Face Interview with Author, December 14, 2023.

Hodgman, John (Owner, Direct Connection Printing & Mailing, www.directconnectionmail.com, 1990–Present). Phone Interview with Author, April 22, 2024.

Jacobs, Larry (Owner, Jacobs Farm/Del Cabo, Inc., www.jacobsfarmdelcabo.com, 1980–Present). Face-to-Face Interview with Author, December 8, 2024.

Johnson, Steve (Owner, Code Welding and Manufacturing Inc., www.codewelding.net, 2005–Present). Face-to-Face Interview with Author, October 13, 2023.

Kubes, Kristine (Owner, Kubes Law Office, PLLC, www.kubeslaw.com, 2009–Present). Face-to-Face Interview with Author, January 22, 2025.

Mackenthun, Cathy (Owner, Mackenthun's Meats & Deli, Inc., www.cathymackenthuns.com, 1981–Present). Face-to-Face Interview with Author, March 18, 2024.

Main, Kelly. 2024. "Top Small Business Statistics." *Forbes Advisor*. www.forbes.com/advisor/business/small-business-statistics

Moser, Myron (Owner, Hartfiel Automation, Inc., www.hartfiel.com, 2000–2021). Face-to-Face Interview with Author, March 27, 2024.

Patrick, James (Owner, Slam Academy Inc., www.slamacademy.com, 2012–Present). Virtual Interview with Author, January 16, 2025.

Rehkamp, Robert (Owner, Robert R. Rehkamp, CPA, 1994–Present). Face-to-Face Interview with Author, January 10, 2025.

Roise, Charlene (Owner, Hess, Roise and Company, Inc., www.hessroise.com, 1990–2020). Face-to-Face Interview with Author, November 14, 2023.

Roise, E-mail Comments to Author, June 24, 2024.

Stock, Sue (Owner, COS, Inc. and BEvera Executive Coaching, www.sue-stock .com, 1997–Present). Face-to-Face Interview with Author, November 9, 2023.

Taplin, Steve. 2024. "Decoding Small Business Failures: Top Four Contributing Factors." *Council Post, Forbes Technology Council.* www.forbes.com /councils/forbestechcouncil/2024/02/27/decoding-small-business-failures -top-four-contributing-factors/

Thompson, Don. (n.d.) "Avoiding the Entrepreneurial Syndrome." *Civil Engineering News*, 24, 26.

Thorp, Paul. January 12, 1999. Memo to Author.

Tutelman, Cary J., and Larry D. Hause. 2008. *The Balance Point*. Famille Press.

Other Resources

The E-Myth Revisited and *Workbook for The E-Myth Revisited* by Michael E. Gerber.

Entrepreneurial Strengths Finder by Jim Clifton.

Johnson O'Conner Research Foundation—Aptitude Testing, www.jocrf.org.

About the Author

Laurie Johnson's professional career includes four decades with Hansen Thorp Pellinen Olson, Inc., a professional services consulting firm in the Minneapolis area. She was a principal owner of the firm for over 25 years and the majority owner for the last 18 years, serving as president of the firm until her retirement in 2023. Throughout her career she has provided technical and management training, including developing and conducting the company's leadership training for future owners.

Index

www.ingramcontent.com/pod-product-compliance
Lightning Source LLC
Chambersburg PA
CBHW061332220326
41599CB00026B/5150